Praise for
The Mother Is Restless and She Doesn't Know Why

'*The Mother Is Restless and She Doesn't Know Why* is a delight of a book – poetic in its sensibility yet with a keen eye for the absurd, and acutely intelligent while also being unafraid of silliness. It is, at its heart, a book about longing and about freedom – and how to reconcile these with the small joys of the everyday, as well as the duties and compromises inherent in love and family life. I never expected to tear through a book about reading Nietzsche – but tear through it I did.'
Fiona Wright, author of *Small Acts of Disappearance*

'Parker has an uncanny gift for writing that embodies the radical fragmentation of our chaotic present. Through flights of reading and social observation, she suggests how the self can cohere despite outside forces demanding our constant attention. By turns hilarious, melancholic, and searching, Parker's debut marks the arrival of a writer of serious talent, intelligence, and compassion.'
Patrick Flanery, author of *The Ginger Child*

'A virtuoso accomplishment. Parker segues effortlessly between the abstract and the personal, the wise and the frivolous.
I rejoiced in such braininess, originality, and wit.'
Anna Goldsworthy, author of *Piano Lessons*

The Mother Is Restless & She Doesn't Know Why

Finding Freedom in the Cage

The Mother Is Restless & She Doesn't Know Why

Finding Freedom in the Cage

Gemma Parker

SCRIBNER

New York · Amsterdam/Antwerp · London · Toronto · Sydney/Melbourne · New Delhi

SCRIBNER

THE MOTHER IS RESTLESS AND SHE DOESN'T KNOW WHY:
FINDING FREEDOM IN THE CAGE

First published in Australia in 2026 by Scribner,
an imprint of Simon & Schuster (Australia) Pty Limited
Level 4, 32 York St, Sydney NSW 2000

New York Amsterdam/Antwerp London Toronto Sydney/Melbourne New Delhi
Visit our website at www.simonandschuster.com.au

SCRIBNER and design are registered trademarks of The Gale Group, Inc.,
used under licence by Simon & Schuster, LLC.

10 9 8 7 6 5 4 3 2 1

© Gemma Parker 2026

Every effort has been made to contact all copyright owners prior to publication of *The Mother Is
Restless and She Doesn't Know Why* to ensure that their contribution is properly acknowledged.
Where we have been unable, despite our best endeavours, to make contact we would welcome
hearing from anyone concerned, so that we may include an appropriate acknowledgement in any
reprints. Please see p. 225 for citation information.

A catalogue record for this
book is available from the
National Library of Australia

9781761636721 (paperback)
9781761636738 (ebook)

Cover design by Alissa Dinallo
Typeset by Midland Typesetters, Australia
Printed and bound in Australia by Griffin Press

The paper this book is printed on is certified against the
Forest Stewardship Council® Standards. Griffin Press holds
chain of custody certification SCS-COC-001185. FSC®
promotes environmentally responsible, socially beneficial
and economically viable management of the world's forests.

Contents

The Journey Out of Nihilism

Your freedom as a writer . . . is life at its most free, if you are fortunate enough to be able to try it, because you select your materials, invent your task, and pace yourself . . . The obverse of this freedom, of course, is that your work is so meaningless, so fully for yourself alone, and so worthless to the world, that no one except you cares whether you do it well, or ever.

– Annie Dillard, *The Writing Life*

BEGINNING

Here is how I start: I read Nietzsche. I read Nietzsche in bed, with a chest cold. I highlight things in green and draw exclamation marks in the margins. I text friends. *You wouldn't expect I could be having so much fun reading Nietzsche*, I tell them. They are worried about their children, about lockdown, about money, about their marriages. I am reading Nietzsche, I repeat. I text them quotes from Nietzsche. They do not reply.

*

I start reading Nietzsche because I cannot do anything else: cannot travel to do research, cannot write in a foreign café. I take a short trip out of the city with my husband and children to stay in Wirrabara Forest, about three hours north. I wake early and read Nietzsche and stare at eucalypts as the sun rises. We take a different route on the drive back, winding through valleys and vineyards. It is so different from our drive out of the city, the Port Wakefield highway flanked by native scrub and acres of blistering samphire, the grey skies blustering and raindrops fat on the windshield. What is it about *returning* that fills me with rage?

RESEARCH

I had originally planned to go back to Paris to research a piece I wanted to write about nihilism, revaluation, and literature. I had lived in Paris as a philosophy student in my early twenties, before kids, before marriage, before teaching. My concept for the piece was vague, but persistent: something about Nietzsche, and artists. Motherhood, and poetry. To write the piece, I knew I needed to go and skulk around my old university on the Left Bank, to lick the cobbled streets to see if I could describe the taste. To find the hotels where Albert Camus wrote his novels; to haunt the old theatres where Samuel Beckett's plays were first performed. I wanted to activate some muscle memory of stalking the cemeteries listening to music, haunting the museums, being bustled through the filthy metro stations. Of gazing at handbags and umbrellas that I would never be able to afford in department store windows. But our borders are closed (imagine writing this a year ago) and I cannot travel. *I cannot write about things because I cannot visit them*, I tell my husband. I try to remember the feel of my boots on cobblestone and the autumn chill of Père Lachaise. It is a waste of time. I don't even like to try to remember.

*

According to Stanley Rosen, 'speech that is indistinguishable from silence is nihilism'. What about a piece that cannot be written? Is that also a type of silence?

SNATCHES

I tell people I'm writing fragments exploring Nietzschean nihilism in life and in literature, but I've come to think of them as *snatches*, rather than fragments. A fragment implies a relationship with a whole, whereas a *snatch* is stolen – swift. It's *whatever can be managed*. That's how I write. At the kitchen table after sweeping away breakfast crumbs. Answering questions, smiling at children, bargaining for another ten minutes. *Snatch* also has an intimate and low-brow female-ness about it that I like, as if my practice can be reduced to gutter-talk. It is defiant, resistant.

It also feels close to hopeless. Nietzsche did not write confined to a small apartment with two young children. This is not how I imagined working: this is not what Virginia Woolf outlined in *A Room of One's Own*. But it's work that is being done, despite the circumstances, and I have to believe this counts for something.

My children interrupt me as I write. 'Can we cut this magazine up for craft?' my daughter asks brightly. I nod as she takes the scissors from the kitchen drawer and calculate that this buys me another fifteen minutes.

*

Once, when I was teaching abroad, a student of mine wore a t-shirt that said *Snatch: The Best Snack in The World*. It was written so that it looked like a vintage logo for a candy bar. 'Sammy,' I asked politely, 'do you know what your t-shirt means?' She flushed. 'Is it bad?' she asked. I paused, debating how to answer, not wanting to embarrass her or to leave her in the dark. Her boyfriend, sitting next to her, quickly pulled up a definition on his phone. 'It means thief!' he told her, cringing. She turned pale. 'Oh, that is bad,' she whispered, while I fought to control my face.

I still enjoy the word snatch because of this duality – its hidden sense of furtive intimacy and hurried theft. This is how I write – I steal moments and do intimate work with a sense of desperation, of urgency. As if it is a heist and I have only thirty seconds to get the jewel. There's a necessary fluidity to working like this. You must always be ready to write, ready to stop. You need the capacity to be in flux, to make something out of nothing, to slip tirelessly between the creative and the domestic.

'We cut out the Battery Bunny with the battery!' my son comes in yelling. 'And now we love him!' my daughter shrieks. They dance gleefully around the kitchen table with the cut-out rabbit. 'We love him, we love him,' they chant. My fifteen minutes are up.

I can't tell you if it is a good way to write. It is the only way I know.

'Tirelessly'! (Eye roll).

Avant-Garde

According to *British Vogue*, Arundhati Roy, upon being offered a place on a writers' retreat, responded with comic alarm: 'Retreat? No! I want to go on an advance!'

Departure

Although the city I live in is far-flung, remote, a significant distance from other major cities, departure is still theoretically simple. You can take the Eastern freeway that leads to the artistic metropolis, the one crowded with saké bars and chic graffiti. You can head south, following a tortuous road flanked by a rocky coastline and a sparkling slate of ocean that unfolds into forests thick with stringy-bark gums and grass trees. Or you can take the northern highway, the one that leads into the remote outback. If you leave the city in this direction, the nearest capital is 2,600 km away. Once you head north, you can continue straight into the sandy deserts or spike west at the top of the gulf, heading out to explore the wild peninsulas or across the vast Nullarbor, Latin for land without trees, a stretch known to the original custodians as Oondiri, 'the waterless'. When they are open, the roads lead out.

The first part of the drive north is a jumble of pawn shops and motels, car yards and intersections. The city dump is in this direction, and the route passes the salt pans, wetlands, and mangroves. The vegetation is a mix of local, native, and imported plants, most from similarly arid plains in Africa, South America and the Middle East. There are some notably ill-fitting displays, like rows of palm trees, cactus, and clumps of bamboo planted as windbreaks or as part of some tropical-exotic aesthetic along the edge of otherwise pitiful properties. The small estuaries that trickle to the coast here are flanked by imposing red gums and long clusters of swamp oaks, and the road soon flattens into a four-lane highway, divided by a wide median strip landscaped with salt bush, east-coast melaleuca, and mallee gums. Then come the samphire salt meadows. Samphire is a low-growing plant that looks like a cross between ocean coral and a desert succulent, with deep red tips that reach skyward, giving the plains a vermilion haze. The foliage becomes more feral as you get away from the city's northern suburbs and towards the head of the gulf. The strips of land either side of the highway have the multilayered canopies of remnant vegetation, land nobody cultivates, discarded and wild and ecstatic.

Fragments

'You don't have to be a poet to be prone to apophenia,' Olivia Laing cautions, 'to seeking meaningful patterns in the scattered, senseless data of the everyday.'

Research (Part II)

So here I am, with my research folder labelled 'Nihilism', supposedly writing about the time I lived in Paris and studied at one of the top *écoles* with a bunch of bourgeois Parisians, but describing samphire instead. Writing about the past makes me feel claustrophobic and cross. What does it matter if I had a huge apartment in Bastille, or that I lived on stale baguettes and powdered leek soup, or that my favourite professor wore crocodile-skin shoes and velvet suits?

Nihilism

I've long been interested in nihilism because I find the concept of a meaningless existence intoxicating, liberating, horrifying – equal parts destructive and generative. Destructive because why continue living, generative because *why continue living?* It's most frequently associated with Nietzsche, with his statement walrus moustache, who used it in countless contradictory ways, as prophecy, as diagnosis, as insult and rapture, as potential salvation. A lot of Nietzsche's writings on nihilism detail the crisis of meaning that Europe faced post-Enlightenment, the 'vacuum of values' that resulted from the rise in faith in science and reason, and the crumbling faith in Christian morals. Nietzsche refers to this crisis as 'the death of god'. But although one can pounce on nihilism as an excuse for anarchy, or yield to the utter despair of it, Nietzsche extols 'the death of god', and the subsequent vacuum of values, as a profound opportunity for 'revaluation':

> Indeed, at hearing the news that 'the old god is dead', we philo-
> sophers and 'free spirits' feel illuminated by a new dawn; our heart
> overflows with gratitude, amazement, forebodings, expectation –
> finally the horizon seems clear again, even if not bright; finally our
> ships may set out again, set out to face any danger; every daring
> of the lover of knowledge is allowed again; the sea, *our* sea, lies
> open again; maybe there has never been such an 'open sea'.

Nietzsche is energetic in detailing the historical events that have led to this crisis of nihilism, but he also presents it as a project – the most vital of all projects – for philosophers and 'free spirits' to consider, not just for society, but for themselves, as individuals. God is dead . . . Our old belief systems no longer apply. The horizon is free again. So now what?

MEDITATION

My friend Nico says that whenever he goes to the doctor in France they listen to his symptoms and then tell him to *drink more water*; whenever I go to the doctor here in Australia they listen to my symptoms and ask if I *practice mindfulness*. Tired of imagining bubbles floating along a river or balloons drifting into the ether, I create my own guided meditation. It goes like this: I am packing a small carry-on suitcase. I pack my Haus of Dizzy earrings first, and then my navy-blue Birkenstocks, my French cotton summer dress, my runners. I place a notebook and the books I am reading (Maggie Nelson's *Bluets* and Sei Shōnagon's *The Pillow Book*) and the books I will read next (Claudia Rankine's *Citizen* and Yoshida Kenkō's *Essays in Idleness*). My yoga mat, my orthopaedic pillow. My grey cashmere jumper, a pair of brown leather boots, two t-shirts, a pair of black jeans, a sports bikini. I fold everything carefully, pressing sharp creases like origami. More earrings – the jade hoops and the Tasmanian ones that look like silver lace. A sky-blue raincoat. A woollen beanie. I take an eyebrow pencil and eyelash curlers, a toothbrush, moisturiser, rosehip oil. Exercise clothes, a hoodie, and finally an apple. I have a slim grey leather wallet with my ID and debit card. Then I go to the airport, stow my carry-on suitcase, take a window seat and imagine I am gazing at the ocean and clouds as we ascend, and I relax into the seat. I imagine I am leaving and will never return.

REVALUATION

The issue, however, as Nietzsche passionately reminds us, is that nobody can adequately answer the question *So now what?* We are too tainted by our various cultures and upbringings, too conditioned by religion and society, to be able to untangle any objective truth or establish any new meaning in the vacuum created by 'the death of god'. Anything we might think is meaningful or of value is just a reiteration of the values we have been raised to believe in. And yet, uncowed by this impossibility, believing in a future for which there is no roadmap, Nietzsche still spends a lot of time describing the *thinker of the future*, the *free spirit*, the one who will be able to establish new values once total nihilism has been realised, or accepted. 'The pure spirit' unfettered by social and cultural conditioning.

The potential for this future philosopher is explored throughout his oeuvre, sometimes in conversational, if ecstatic, tones, and other times in extended metaphors that lend his work a sort of prophetic, visionary conceit. Most iterations involve destruction before creation can take place, an obliteration of what has come before. My favourite description of the evolution required to overcome the nihilistic times in which we live is in Nietzsche's 'Three Metamorphoses' in *Thus Spoke Zarathustra*. This metamorphosis begins with the camel, studious and reverent, weighed down by knowledge and obedience to scripture. The camel then must become the lion, who roaringly renounces all duty and thus liberates itself from loyalty to all past values and dogmas. The lion comes before the child, who sees everything with clarity and innocence, and is thus able to establish its own will and values.

For obvious reasons, I am sick of the child. The lion is incapable, Nietzsche writes, of the state of being, or mindset, required to create new values. 'But to create itself freedom for new creation,' he tells us, 'that the might of the lion can do.'

LACK

In French, the verb *se manquer*, which means 'to miss', operates differently to its equivalent in English. To say *I miss you* in French you must say *tu me manques*, which could be translated literally as *you create missing in me*, or, *you I am lacking*. I fumble this verb regularly, rerouting it as *je te manque*, but that just means *you miss me*, or *I create in you the feeling of missing me*. I struggle to accept that missing can be passive – something that is done by another. In English it is active, subjective, we are in control, we are *missing*. In French, it always feels to me as if the other has left, the void carved out against our will.

I dislike expressing a missing, a lack, that is done to me. It makes me feel as if I am hollowed out; I am made concave, and my only choice is to reshape around the void, as if the black hole itself is a skeleton, is architecture.

LIBERATION

The lion cannot create new values, Nietzsche writes, but it can be involved in the liberation of the human spirit from its fidelity to all those who have shaped it. He sees this liberation as both necessary and violent, a revolution. Nietzsche writes a lot about the desire for freedom, about shaking off chains and shackles, obligations and loyalties. In *Human, All Too Human*, he explains:

> The great liberation comes for those who are thus fettered suddenly, like the shock of an earthquake . . . a will and desire awakens to go off, anywhere, at any cost; a vehement dangerous curiosity for an undiscovered world flames and flickers in all its senses. 'Better to die than to go on living *here*' – thus responds the imperious voice and temptation: and this 'here', this 'at home' is everything it had hitherto loved!

A will and desire awakens to go off, anywhere, at any cost. I've spent my life living with this desire, the opposite of *homesickness*, the constant longing to flee. Farsickness. Not always to be admired. Nietzsche describes it like this:

> a rebellious, arbitrary, volcanically erupting desire for travel, strange places, estrangements, coldness, soberness, frost . . . an enigmatic, question-packed, questionable victory.

A questionable victory! 'Nihilism does not only contemplate the "in vain!" nor is it merely the belief that everything deserves to perish: one helps to destroy . . .' Nietzsche wrote in his final years. Meaning, as I choose to understand it, that you cannot simply wait to become the lion: you must be actively engaged in clearing out the space necessary for new ideas, new creations.

Maybe he didn't mean it like this. It is hard to write about Nietzsche. Reading him one can feel, deeply, the resonance of his ideas only to find they refuse to be held in place, they defy any comprehensive explanation. It is also standard among scholars of philosophy to mention that his sanity was questionable towards the end of his life – that his final work, from which I have just quoted, is a posthumous collation of notebooks published after his complete breakdown (the thing with the horse). But so much of Nietzsche's writings seem wild and erratic to me, that's part of their poetic appeal, as if he is striving to contain madness, the moment right before insanity renders everything incomprehensible, indecipherable, inexplicable – voiceless.

FERNWEH

Fernweh is the German word that means *a longing for far-off places*, in particular those we do not know or have yet to experience. A longing for an unknown place, a yearning for elsewhere. Farsickness. In English sometimes we borrow the other German word for wanting to travel, *wanderlust*. The difference between *wanderlust* and *Fernweh* is that one expresses desire and the other gives voice to ache. One speaks of want, the other of lack.

Fern means far and *wehe* means woe, pain, or misery. Longing as a wound, an illness, an inexplicable and violent abyss. Its opposite is *heimweh*, homesickness. Portuguese has a word, *saudade*, which translates roughly as *the presence of absence*, and it hinges on the same pain: the consciousness of lack, the inadequacy of now. I was born with *Fernweh*, the desire to leave. Is it genetic, or is it just an origin myth – a *pourquoi* story?

LACK (PART II)

'Are poems written on such themes as "Going to view the cherry blossoms only to find they had scattered" or "On being prevented from visiting the blossoms" inferior to those on "Seeing the blossoms"?' Kenkō asks. Does it take the heart of a 12th-century Buddhist hermit to find beauty in the pain of missing things, of losing things, of being denied something that you long for?

Think of my son, four years old, coasting down a gentle slope on his bicycle home from kindergarten. It is a warm spring day, and he has a mouth full of M&Ms. 'I'm not really happy,' he says, turning to me.

BROKEN

'The thing with the horse' happened in 1889 while Nietzsche was living in Turin, where he wrote *Ecce Homo*, his famously eccentric autobiography (one of my favourite lines from an earlier work states that all philosophy is 'a type of involuntary and unselfconscious memoir', so of course *Ecce Homo*, his voluntary and self-aware memoir, is bizarre, bombastic and full of lies). Apparently, seeing a man whipping his horse, Nietzsche approached and threw his arms around the animal's neck in agitation, chastising the man for his cruelty. This moment is said to be significant because Nietzsche never recovered – this taxing, emotional experience was the definitive trigger that led to a complete and irrevocable psychological collapse. After this public outburst, he continued to live, inarticulate and uncomprehending, until his death ten years later.

The Plaza Carlo Alberto in Turin, right next to Nietzsche's apartment, has a statue of a man on a horse that was erected in 1861. This is not unusual – lots of squares in Europe have a man on a horse, brandishing a sword. But whenever I think of this story, I imagine Nietzsche, broken by his years of intense thought, study, and illness, hallucinating the cruel scene and clambering up to wrap his arms around the neck of the equestrian statue, weeping.

RESEARCH (PART III)

I take a drive to Port Wakefield with one of my husband's musician friends who makes a living clearing invasive plant species from public areas, parklands, and riverbanks. 'You can't go to Paris,' my husband shrugs, 'but you can still drive to Port Wakefield with Bob in one of the shitty cars he keeps in his front yard.'

'As a nonfiction writer you must get on the plane,' William Zinsser counsels in *On Writing Well*. On the way to see Bob I get stuck in traffic behind a bus that has *Travel Here This Year!* emblazoned on it, with the word *Here* snugly shaped into a map of Australia. I snort to myself. As if we have a choice! When I arrive at Bob's house, I spend some time drinking a scalding hot cup of coffee in the front room, looking at a shelf of books propped above the piano bookended by sheep skulls. He points out a book about plants he has just read. 'I can't recommend it to you,' he says. 'It's no good; the writer gets heaps of stuff wrong.'

DEPARTURE (PART II)

After her adoptive mother died when my mother was young, she was in a car crash that resulted in months of reconstructive surgery, and then she left her hometown in New Zealand and never returned. At nineteen she flew to Australia on a one-way ticket. I've heard the story of her journey so many times I can quote it word for word. 'I had a one-way ticket to Western Australia and $100 in my pocket. At a stopover in Sydney, I spent $96 on clothes at the Sydney markets, so I only had $4 left, but that was all I needed – enough for two packets of smokes.'

RIDDLES

The thinker of the future, according to Nietzsche, will have 'What Do I Matter!' pinned above his door. Nietzsche is scathing about philosophers in general, writing that their goal is to establish 'the knowability of things' so they can compress the world into a solvable riddle they alone can be credited with 'unriddling'.

Next to my desk I have pinned a copy of Suji Kwock Kim's poem 'Monologue for an Onion'. Kim's poem is satisfyingly brutal:

Look at you, chopping and weeping. Idiot.
Is this the way you go through life, your mind
A stopless knife, driven by your fantasy of truth,

Of lasting union – slashing away skin after skin
From things, ruin and tears your only signs
Of progress? Enough is enough.

A stopless knife. I joke to my husband that I think the poem is really about my project, quoting the third to last stanza:

> . . . You are the one
> In pieces. Whatever you meant to love, in meaning to
> You changed yourself

The poem comes from Kim's collection *Notes from the Divided Country*, which is so beautiful and violent that I could not, in fact, bear it. The poems I read stay with me like awkward ghosts, unsure of how to haunt me. I hug the book to my chest before placing it in the library return shoot, as if to say to the poems that I am sorry I could not take care of them. Was I afraid that, by meaning to love them, I would change myself?

ELSEWHERE

The same feeling of not belonging, of futility, wherever I go: I pretend interest in what matters nothing to me . . . What attracts me is elsewhere, and I don't know where that elsewhere is.

— Emil Cioran, *The Trouble with Being Born*

The Journey Out of Nihilism

A significant journey, my dad wrote to me of nihilism, when I was twenty and obsessed. *The trip back even more interesting.* The trip back from nihilism, he told me, is what one decides to do once they've decided there's nothing, objectively, worth doing. How we return from the abyss. How we keep going. It is this I think of when I come across Anne Lamott explaining Samuel Beckett's famous nihilism: he didn't kill himself. He wrote.

Research (Part IV)

Bob has a long beard and a collection of old, beat-up utes. As we drive, he tells me that there is a difference between native and local provenance flora, between foreign species that thrive in South Australia and things that originate here. He points out patches of native landscaping as we cross bridges and merge onto highways that have been planted with Australian bushes and flowers, explaining that many of the species are not actually local. They are just native to some part of this sprawling continent. I tell him I often mistakenly think of foreign species as natives, because they grow so well here, like salvia, with its bouquets of fierce purple, deep red, soft pink, and dusty blue. As if anything that grows well in this harsh, dry climate must have originated here. Bob says that these types of plants are precisely what in his profession is classed as a weed – that which thrives, strangling out the natives.

Bob tells me about the different plants, explains the genus and their status and whether or not the areas in which they are growing have been cultivated, protected, or are just wild patches of land nobody cares for. We stand on the edge of the highway as the trucks shriek past us and he pulls down sheoak buds for me to inspect. 'I am sick of hearing about how people feel they don't belong,' says Bob suddenly. 'Nobody belongs. None of us belong anywhere.'

PARIS

In Paris a friend of a friend came to stay with me, and asked one morning what I was studying. I offered a long, excited answer about architecture, socialism, jazz, theories of justice, nihilism, terrorism, and autoethnography, and he captioned a photo of me on his blog with *In Paris I am staying with Gemma, who is studying Everything.*

A more straightforward answer would have been that I was studying philosophy, or political theory, loosely defined, but neither of those terms seemed to cut it. I was at a Political Science university but my courses had wild and poetic names like 'Cultural Triangulations' and 'The Sociology of Jazz'. The course I think about most often was called 'Nihilism, Apocalypse, and Disenchantment: Myths of Rupture, Ideologies of "The End"'. As soon as I saw it in my course planner I felt my heart flip; I felt a part of me ignite.

I'm cupping my hand around that tiny flame now, trying to coax it back to life. It feels so fragile, so close to being extinguished, it makes me want to weep.

RESEARCH (PART V)

'There is not a steel divider that separates what is domestic from what is not,' David Bellos says in his 2020 W.G. Sebald Lecture, which I watch on Zoom because we are all in lockdown and I cannot travel to Paris to do my research.

REVALUATION (PART II)

It is not enough simply to accept the essential nihilistic absurdity of the world, according to Nietzsche. Philosophers should seek the full metamorphosis that is required before they can confidently propose meaning or value to our lives. Before new values can be proposed, the *conditions* must be met. The philosopher must be ready to *destroy*, to *obliterate*, to sweep the stage. To make space for a new way of seeing the world, of knowing oneself.

CONDITIONS

The formula for happiness, someone once said, is expectation divided by reality. Probably one of the French pessimists, advocating for low expectations. I married a Frenchman, but a joyous one, a lustful extrovert with the heart of an outlaw. In every city we live he becomes known at the local café or bakery as *the one who likes cakes*, which he always eats like a giant, in three quick bites. He agrees with this formula, but does not lower his expectations, instead forcing reality up to meet them.

One afternoon the children are with their grandparents, and we drive into the countryside to have lunch at an organic farm. Guillaume orders red wine, chicken liver pâté, a steak, and tiramisu. I order vegetarian arancini and pale, fresh cod. I don't drink: I am practising sobriety partly because I have been reading too much Nietzsche and partly because I can't shake this chest cold. The sight of my meal next to a cup of tap water is pitiful, as if I am abstaining. 'I hope you get gout,' I tell my husband bitterly.

*

Guillaume does not get gout; my chest cold lingers.

Now what food do we feed women as artists upon? I asked, remembering, I suppose, that dinner of prunes and custard.

– Virginia Woolf, *A Room of One's Own*

Paris (Part II)

My nihilism professor had slicked-back hair and wore crushed red velvet suits and crocodile-skin shoes. His lectures always sounded like he had typed them up at 4 am after taking LSD and reading Baudrillard. The first time he sat down in our class he rolled his eyes at us and said, 'No fucking laptops. I know what you do on your laptops. If you want to take notes in my class, you take them by hand.' I filled notebook after notebook with the slick poetry of his rants, scattered with quotes from Nietzsche and Durkheim, Cioran and Kojève. I read ravenously, tumbling into subterranean rabbit holes about 'the fatal sensibility' and 'the myth of progress'. I'd never studied anything like it. I was so naïve that in my notes I spell Heidegger H-A-E-D-E-G-E-R and Deleuze D-E-L-O-U-S-E, as in, what you do to get rid of lice.

Questions

If you can manage to stay curious within nihilism's absolute negation of existing value systems and dogmas you might begin to ask a few questions. Those questions might be about the potential for new values, new meaning, discovering new reasons and ways of being, establishing purpose. Those questions might, especially if you are reading a lot of Nietzsche, be about purity. How can I be sure that what I decide now to be of value is not just the voice of my socially and culturally conditioned self, reiterating that which is most acceptable, most comfortable, that which will not be a threat to my belonging? Is this even possible? Questions like this might lead to a longing for obliteration, of sorts, of destruction. Of clearing away everything that has built you. A gutting. A rage of space, unsure even of whether it should be filled.

NIHILISM (PART II)

My Dad's comment regarding the trip back from nihilism was part of an email exchange about my birth certificate, which the French authorities wanted for my student visa in Paris. In response to my enquiry, my father wrote, *I know nothing about your birth certificate, surely your passport is enough . . . Some people come from countries where people are born without certificates, living and dying are deemed sufficient evidence of birth.* It wasn't enough for French bureaucracy, which did not care that I had been raised to be dismissive of historical documents, as if they could tell us anything of who we were, where we had come from. I had to pay for a new certificate to be sent to my large apartment in Bastille, where I sat smoking rolled cigarettes on the sill of the casement window, watching the synchronised legs of women doing Pilates in the expensive studio across the cobbled street.

CONDITIONS (PART II)

My daughter is surly, wretched, and weepy all morning. I finally kneel in front of her on the walk to school to ask if she wants to stay at home. She is in her school uniform, her lunch is packed, and two big tears roll down her cheeks as she nods, 'I want to, yes.' I tuck her into bed with some inky pens and a new sketchbook. 'I have to work,' I tell her.

When I was a teenager, after my parents divorced, my father never forced me to go to school. He'd stick his head in the door to say, 'It's time to go to school,' and I'd reply, 'Not today,' and he would shut the door and call the school without any follow-up questions for me. Even then I thought of his parenting as a type of negative capability, unruffled by contradiction, variety, the impossibility of youth.

LINEAGE

My parents met in the 1970s in Newman, Western Australia, a mining town where they were both employed. This was not a logical destination for either of them. Both had ended up there after busting out of lives that no longer appealed to them, lives that had grown constrictive, predictable, baffling. Neither had particularly clear origins – nothing to necessarily tether them in place. My mother had been adopted by a woman who died when she was young; my father's mother had been orphaned and his father disowned by his Plymouth Brethren family for the unforgiveable sin of marrying a Catholic. Reasons I have no connection to my origins: death, renunciation, rebellion – and romance.

It is hard to write about your parents and grandparents without sounding like a bore. (*What do[es where] I [come from] matter!*) As if these stories will hold you to the page. As if we are drunk and I am telling you of their wildness with frenetic glee.

MAXIMS AND ARROWS

I use my phone to email ideas to myself, to look at when I can get back to my writing. One is a quote from my father, responding to my adolescent brag that I had passed a maths test without studying. 'There's no glory in effortless success,' he had said dismissively, and I tap it into my phone as I remember it, in the middle of making school lunches. Later, when I open this email from myself, my inbox suggests autoreplies: 'True,' 'I see,' and 'What do you mean?'

POET

Sometimes when I tell people that I'm a poet I see them receive this information as stanzas and metaphors, as if they think I am someone who looks carefully at birds. When what I mean is that I live with torrential despair, a torn heart, a restless void. I'm a Steppenwolf, I think of saying instead, a twice hidden beast: once under the mantle of human, and then again as a suburban wife.

PARIS (PART III)

I was so committed to my studies in Paris that on my twenty-fifth birthday, in freezing cold December, I went to a conference about Durkheim at some random *école* in the suburbs. It was surprisingly mediocre, with coffee in paper cups and a dozen nervous people reading from single-spaced A4 papers while the others nodded or frowned. My flatmate was bewildered by my choices, living in the centre of Paris and yet constantly ensconced in the casement windowsill, devouring depressing philosophy. But in contrast to the Durkheim conference, classes at my university on the Left Bank were *electric*. Each week my nihilism professor sat down at his desk and set fire to everything I knew with poetic, bombastic theories diagnosing the apocalyptic disorder of modernity. The narratives of demise that he unfolded were both thrilling and bewildering, disconnected dystopias woven into a saga of dread. 'We are in,' I remember him announcing magnificently, 'the *Kali Yuga* – the age of darkness, and decline.'

LONGINGS

'In the sixteenth century,' writes Sabrina Orah Mark, 'there was a widespread belief that if a pregnant woman's cravings weren't satisfied, the shape of whatever she craved would appear on her newborn. Birthmarks are called *voglie* in Italian, which means longings.' My left foot has a birthmark, a dark pink stain like a slap mark left on the arch. The shape of it is hard to discern, but because of its position I've always thought of it as my mother's longing to travel, imprinted on my skin. I can only presume it was travel. The older I get the more I wonder about other unmet cravings, other pregnant longings that were not satisfied. What else could be stamped so artfully on the arch of the foot?

'I looked,' said my friend Nico, after he met my baby daughter for the first time, 'to see if she has your birthmark. But she doesn't,' he added helpfully, as if I did not know.

DEPARTURE (PART III)

Here's another story of departure: the first time my dad left Adelaide, at the age of twenty, it was a riotous disaster. The combi van he'd bought with a friend broke down soon after they left the city. 'The engine was fucked,' my dad says mildly. 'Did you get conned?' I ask.

'Oh yeah,' he laughs. 'It had been sold to us by a crook, he'd loaded the engine up with grease and oil. My mate had this magnum of champagne that he'd brought along for us to drink the first time the van broke down, so there we were on our first day, drinking hot champagne out of a magnum bottle on the side of the road to Whyalla.'

He made a phone call from Whyalla to his workplace to tell them he wouldn't be coming in, not that day, in fact not ever again.

My dad got a job on the spot as a greaser in an iron ore mine called Iron Baron, just west of Whyalla. The greaser, equipped with a dunny brush and a bucket of grease, climbs up on the boom of the shovels that dig the ore out of the ground. It's the greaser's job to slap the grease into the teeth of the stick, which the operator winds back and forth to distribute the grease along the shaft. The greaser also moves the cables around, heavy electrical cables as thick as a man's arm. I write this in the present tense as if greasers still haul buckets of grease and hurl cables out of the way as shovels scratch iron ore out of the earth, but truly I don't know. All I can tell you is what he told me. 'I read a lot in those days,' he says. 'John Steinbeck, James Baldwin, Angela Davis.' 'What did you read before that?' I ask him. 'Well, I was working in computer programming, so mostly Nietzsche,' he replies.

Dad goes from programming computers and wearing a suit to greasing the shaft of an iron ore shovel like this: he leaves one night, convinced that there is more to life than the binary he is being offered. The revolutionary spirit of the times had collapsed into drugs and alcohol, and the alternative was the traditional suburban career, marriage, and kids. 'Alcohol can make you brave,' he tells me, 'but you have to take that bravery out into the real world for it to mean anything. At some point you have to decide if you are the sort of person who sits around drinking and talking about what you are going to do, or if you are going to actually do it.'

He found something in Whyalla, a glimpse of a world that was more real than anything he had been exposed to before. The migrant workers – many of whom were from Yugoslavia and who knew of danger, and hard work – were as foreign to him as the physical fatigue and disorientation of shift work. He was getting closer to what he thought of as the real. This was not just an adventure – this was a necessity. 'The place was full of whackos,' he says. 'Full of the poetry of just about every different type of person, the liberation of variety. There was no template or path for who to be.'

He left friends, family, a lover, his studies, his job, slamming the door shut on any predetermined destiny or potential future. 'You can't leave doors ajar,' he tells me. 'It doesn't do much for your soul.'

FRAGMENTS (PART II)

It is a strange experience to be writing fragments about meaning and to fear, constantly, that what you are making is actually meaningless. Just a bunch of unfinished scraps.

TRUCKS

Later my dad progressed from being a greaser to driving dump trucks. Many drivers took books with them because there was nothing to do while the truck was being loaded, and that could take up to twenty minutes, depending on how hard the digging was. You'd wait around for the shovel operator to toot his horn as a sign that you should be off. During that waiting time, Dad says, just about everybody used to read. Most people read cowboy stories, collections of pulp fiction that were left in the trucks for the next driver. He tells me that he read more at that point than he had for years. 'I guess there weren't many distractions,' I say, thinking of mobile phones. 'Yeah, other than that you might die,' he replies.

The trucks were backed up under the shovel to get loaded with iron ore, which was blasted into small, loose pieces by explosives. A siren blared out over the site to tell the workers to turn the machinery off because they were about to set off explosives. It's eerie, my dad says, because everyone has to stop work at the same time, so the mine goes from being rowdy and noisy with trucks to suddenly being dead quiet. The shovels all swing around so that they have their backs to the blast to minimise any damage. Workers in the mine stayed in their shovels. No-one was qualified, he says. There were no drug and alcohol tests, no safety procedures. In charge of explosives was a Czech guy called Shorty. There were no detonators – Shorty had to physically light a fuse, and then drive his truck away from the blast. Once, my dad tells me, the truck wouldn't start. In the deadly stillness of the mine all they could hear was the impotent whir of the engine. They held their breath. They heard Shorty swear. Finally the engine leapt to life and Shorty bolted away from the diminishing fuse, his truck pummelled by debris as the explosion tore ore out of the earth. This was the sort of cowboy shit that happened in those days, Dad says.

PRECONDITIONS

Nietzsche writes that the preconditions of the philosopher's task are that one must perhaps have been 'a critic and a skeptic and a dogmatist and historian and, moreover, a poet and collector and traveller and guesser of riddles and moralist and seer and "free spirit" and practically everything, in order to run through the range of human values and value feelings and *be able* to gaze with many eyes and consciences from the heights into every distance . . .' You can pursue these preconditions forever, of course, before you ever get to philosophising. I can tell you firsthand it's not the worst way to live.

DEPARTURE (PART IV)

After years in different mining towns, my dad journeyed east to London – that's another departure I've heard a lot about. 'What type of boat was it?' I ask. 'It was a fucking old boat,' my dad replies. The cheapest cabins were $450 and there were no windows, with eight men in a room. It took around five weeks to get to London from Sydney, squeezing through the Panama Canal and some of the roughest ports in the world. He met some shearers on the boat who were heading to Florida to shear sheep – three brothers, big, boozy men who were constantly in trouble and locked up in the hold of the boat every second night for pulling drunken stunts like trying to climb up into the crow's nest. He tells me they were from Queensland, and I picture them striding through flood waters with young calves across their shoulders. Tropical storms and droughts had raised these men – as if they cared for man-made rules, as if they would respect frail, human authority.

*

Europe was a watery disappointment, full of more of what he had tried to leave behind, wasted hippies and strait-laced programmers. He loped off instead for a trip overland back to Australia, through Greece, Turkey, and Iran. The further east he travelled, the more alive he felt. There was a sense of possibility, of chaos and a bright unpredictability. 'A bus in Germany was just a bus with nice seats,' he says. 'By the time I was in India the bus had no seats and they drove across the desert with the headlights off because they were trying to avoid curfew. In Pakistan we were on a bus and a camel caravan arrived out of the desert to offer us hot tea and ask if we wanted to exchange any money – the guy had a bag full of cash strapped to the camel, and he knew the exact exchange rate that day.'

LIBRARIES

I have a green cloth-bound hardcover reference book that comprehensively lists all of Virginia Woolf's direct and inferred sources. Woolf was famously well-read. 'Best of all was her father's permission, freely given, to use his "large and quite unexpurgated" library,' the author writes. 'As a result, from early years, her diaries and letters are dotted with references to books she is reading.'

When I was growing up, we had one bookcase and it was filled with dusty paperbacks that looked almost identical – yellow Picador spines cracked in the middle, the brittle pages tinged a reddish brown. 'We used to read in the trucks, so they're all pretty filthy,' Dad said when I complained that they stained my hands when I read them. The fine red particles of dust from the mining towns had stayed trapped between the pages. Bull dust, they call it, 'a fine red aeolian dust especially common in the Australian outback,' and

28

a term that has also come to mean *bullshit*, meaning nonsense, or rubbish.

Did this really happen? Did I really have stained palms as I palmed through Hermann Hesse and Hunter S. Thompson? *Stop telling me the story about the red mining town dust staining your hands*, a high-school friend wrote inside a book she gave me for my birthday, a brand new copy of *Zen and the Art of Motorcycle Maintenance* with crisp white pages. But now when I look at the few books I have kept I cannot find any evidence of the dust at all, just faded pages and grubby spines.

Bull dust can be deadly. It can settle into large potholes as a fine silt, like quicksand, deceiving drivers into believing that the road is flat. Travelling along an outback road, a vehicle can suddenly lurch into a craterous ditch, disguised by flimsy dust. Like a reverse mirage – what the desert is hiding.

Herman Hesse

'What does "Steppenwolf" mean?' my husband asks. I slide my eyes over to look at him in the driver's seat, but he remains unchanged: the same large, straightforward man I married. There is no chance that he has been flicking through my writings late at night, picking through my private thoughts, wondering why his wife calls herself a *twice hidden beast*. I ramble a reply, Hermann Hesse blah blah, a creature that is not quite man, that is wild, but forced to live by the rules of polite society. 'Why do you ask?' 'It's the name of the band,' he gestures towards the radio, 'Born to be Wild' roaring out at us.

*

Steppenwolf, steppenwife, steppenmère.

Hesse, in a piece he refers to as a 'conjectural biography' written by an imaginary future version of himself, wrote that from the age of thirteen onwards, he wanted to be a poet, 'or nothing at all'. Once he had decided upon this future, however, he had to contend with the realisation that there was no way to learn to be a poet – no pathway, no schools, courses, or professional training one might undertake as an apprentice of poetry, as one could to train to become 'a teacher, minister, doctor, mechanic, merchant, post-office employee, or a musician, painter, architect'. Despite the honour given to poets (usually, he notes, posthumously), becoming one was impossible, and wanting to be one was both ridiculous, and shameful. Hesse explains:

> I had quickly learned what there was to be learned from the situation: a poet was simply something you were allowed to be but not to become . . . Thus I saw between me and my distant goal nothing but abysses yawning; everything was uncertain, everything devoid of value, only one thing remained constant: that I intended to become a poet, whether that turned out to be easy or hard, ridiculous or creditable.

Departure (Part V)

So I was raised with stories of leaving, raised to leave, raised to raze it all and to lean into the thrill of anonymity. Like both parents I also left on one-way tickets, shucking off my life like a tiresome, ill-fitting coat. Often these escapes were paired with break-ups, as if my love affairs were stitched into the fabric of the landscape I was leaving. It was addictive, almost – the sense of unbuckling, unstrapping, unspooling, the naked glee of being alone in a window seat, gazing down at clouds and ocean with a frenetic sense of irrelevance. My flight to Paris was one of these great, terrible sheddings. The skin of my life had grown too tight, ready to be peeled off in one diaphanous casing. I'd had fights with people I loved, I had become engrossed in an impossible relationship, and once I was on the plane *none of it mattered*, I was just a strange solitary figure on a stopover in Kuala Lumpur, feeling the fragmentary charm of being anonymous, being nobody.

LIBRARIES (PART II)

I cannot find my copy of *Thus Spoke Zarathustra*. I do not own a lot of books – twelve shelves of approximately fifty books each, shabby hardcovers with sticky-taped spines, Penguin paperbacks, skinny poetry titles and hefty collected works, over-read classics, dusty Picadors and shiny new trade paperbacks. I have signed first editions, and about a hundred books I have not read. They are not organised in any order. Some I hated; some I bought thinking I was someone else. Some are copies of the same book in different languages, some are different editions of the same original. Some cost a lot of money, were hard to track down, had to be imported, and I still have not read them. Most of it is very serious literature, melancholy, political. I have a surprising number of books about Bob Dylan, none of which are very good. The portrait that my bookshelves build of me feels unfamiliar, inconsistent, and haphazard. My library doesn't look curated but it has been obsessively culled. Each time I moved overseas I whittled it down to fit into boxes I could safely and unobtrusively store in the garages of family and friends. That is why so many of the books are unread – my bookcase is not a performance, it is a proposal. A potential self, waiting with a jittery knee.

*

I text Nico. *You're the only one I would have lent it to*, I say. He replies at his 6 am, drinking coffee and rolling himself a cigarette in his apartment in Strasbourg. *It's in a box*, he says. *Do you need it?*

No, I say. *I just wanted to know where it was.*

It's important to note that 'obsessively culled' does not mean better. Culling is not always linked to refinement.

RESEARCH (PART VI)

As we drive, Bob lists the plants he can see along the side of the highway, and I write them down one after the other in a little red notebook, trying to capture his sidelong remarks at the same time. At the Port Wakefield pub, we have a dark ale in the sun and chat to the owners, who are old friends of Bob's. He explains that we are driving because I am a writer, and everybody accepts this without question.

CLOSURE

In *Hiking with Nietzsche*, hiker and philosopher John Kaag tells us that Nietzsche's philosophy is no 'mere abstraction'. His is not the sort of philosophy we should engage in sitting comfortably in an armchair at home. 'One needs to physically rise, stand up, stretch, and set off,' Kaag says. 'This transformation occurs, according to Nietzsche, in a "sudden sentience and prescience of the future, of near adventures, of seas open once more, and aims once more permitted and believed in."'

But when will the seas be open once more?

Paris (Part IV)

Each student had to do an oral presentation on one of the topics for our course. The student given the topic of 'nihilism' came after me, alphabetically ('Nietzsche'). I worried that I'd gone rogue with a talk that ranged from Dostoyevsky to Dylan, but the nihilism guy spent his five minutes with his feet up on a desk, playing Richard Strauss's 'Thus Spoke Zarathustra' as he ate two bananas, one after the other.

Dionysus

'Poor Clothilde,' my niece sighs heavily one night. 'We all have to do a presentation on a Greek god, and she got *Dionysus*.' I glance at her, bemused. 'He's the worst,' she explains. 'He's like the Mad Hatter of Greek mythology.'

I wrote an essay about Dionysus for another course I took in Paris that became the foundation for my dissertation on suicide terrorism. I realised too late that I was more interested in Euripides' *The Bacchae* than I was in the sickening and destabilising tactics of war. Dionysus, god of wine, fertility, vegetation and ecstasy appears in *The Bacchae* as the ultimate antagonist. In Euripides' play, King Pentheus suffers the horrific fate of being torn limb from limb by his mother Agave, who, in a Dionysian frenzy, is convinced that he is a lion. At the beginning of the play, the women of Thebes, including Agave and her sisters, have been bewitched by the part-man, part-God into a state of ecstatic delirium, and are worshipping Dionysus in the mountains. The fate of Pentheus is the excessive and violent revenge of Dionysus, for the young king's obstinate refusal to recognise Dionysus' legitimacy as a god. 'The paradoxical nature of Dionysus, considered something of an arch-villain among Greek gods, highlights the tenuous binaries that are at the heart of our societies, our political systems and ultimately ourselves,' I wrote in my essay. And later, 'Creation necessitates destruction, and that which is formed contains the seeds of its own unforming.'

SCORN

When my studies in Paris ended, my nihilism professor asked about my plans for the future. 'I'm going to have babies and write poetry,' I replied blithely, and he looked at me with scorn. I'll never forget that moment, because my reaction to his scorn was my own scorn, magnified. It was so brutal that it felt comic, cartoonish, wildly disproportionate. As if he had rolled his eyes at me and I had dropped a hundred-kilogram anvil that punched him six feet into the earth. As if he had elbowed me in frustration and I had turned a flamethrower on him that charred him to his skeleton. As if he had said my curtains were ugly, and I had come back with a bulldozer and flattened his fucking house. So outsized, so over-the-top, so overwhelmingly uncharacteristic was my scorn in response to his scorn that I may or may not have laughed in his face.

I did not feel a shred of shame or embarrassment. All I felt was that he had, somehow – my beloved professor! – *missed the fucking point* of nihilism. His reaction to my decision to drop out of academia and become a mother and a poet was fucking *scorn*, when *he* was the one who had missed the provocation at the heart of it all, the exhortation to *look into the abyss* and *become who you are.* I had not spent a semester reading Nietzsche and Durkheim and Cioran and Baudrillard for nothing. Destruction, anomie, apocalypse, despair, nihilism. What was he doing with these texts, if he was not stacking up his reality against the dystopia of modernity and asking himself how he could live in such a world? It was he who had posed the question, during the lecture on Baudrillard – 'What do you do, after the Dionysian orgy. What do you do when every day is an orgy?' What, indeed?

What felt especially stupid about his scorn was that I wasn't even particularly original! I was dropping out in the name of love and family and *art*, for fuck's sake. And of all art, it was not even something off-beat or particularly radical! *Poetry!* What was Nietzsche advocating if it wasn't for a future of *poetics* and *creativity*?

> Art . . . alone knows how to turn these nauseous thoughts about the horror or absurdity of existence into notions with which one can live: these are the *sublime* as the artistic taming of the horrible, and the *comic* as the artistic discharge of the nausea of absurdity.

How could the end point of apocalyptic enquiry be academia, over birth, passion, and poetics? Was the point of it all just to teach, publish, get tenure? *Why the hell did you spend so much time talking about Kali Yuga?* I wanted to ask. *What did you think you were teaching us?* How could the answer have ever been *more study?* More of that Durkheim conference? What kind of radical fucking revaluation was that?

IKIGAI

My favourite point of Nietzsche's is in *The Wanderer and His Shadow*, where he writes that freedom of will is a delusion, but most people don't realise it because we pretend that what our character obliges us to do is in fact what we want to do. 'It is as if the silkworm sought the freedom of its will in spinning,' he writes. People feel themselves most free where their '*feeling of living* is greatest'. I love this phrase – the *feeling of living.* 'That through which the individual human being is strong,' Nietzsche continues, 'wherein he feels himself animated, he involuntarily thinks must also always be the element of his freedom: he accounts dependence and dullness, independence and the feeling of living as necessarily coupled.'

I know where my *feeling of living* is greatest – in leaving and in writing. The reason I like this point so much is because I do not feel, necessarily, that I want to leave, or to write, but rather that I am *obliged* to do these things, that they are a need that cannot be negotiated with, and that in doing them I am sating some internal beast that would otherwise wreak havoc. That has – I should be honest here – that *has* wreaked havoc. The freedom I feel in doing these things is the relief of a smoker who, inhaling, feels the sudden silencing of a relentless addiction.

I lived for many, many years in a state of agitated withdrawal. I speak to a friend in Japan who witnessed parts of this multi-stage unravelling when we lived in the same apartment block in Osaka. I tell her that I'm doing better now, that writing is my *ikigai.* I do not know a lot of Japanese, but this phrase, meaning 'reason for being', has immediate utility – she lights up and scrambles around on her desk to find a complicated spreadsheet she is working on. 'This is my ikigai!' she moans comically, holding it up to the screen for me to see.

SMOKING

When I met my husband he smoked skinny brown cigarettes that he rolled with liquorice rolling paper and wads of loose tobacco. He told me that he would never quit, that smoking had saved his life. After bogging his quad bike in mud whilst mustering cattle in the far North of Australia, he had made a fire with the lighter he carried and was able to dry his clothes and keep warm as the desert night temperatures dropped to near freezing. My grandfather, my father's father, also believed that smoking had saved his life. During WWII, while training to be a pilot, the plane he was in nose-dived and crashed. Everyone was killed except my grandfather, who had been at the back of the plane smoking a cigarette at the time. He smoked two packs a day until he died of lung cancer at the age of sixty.

My husband quit smoking soon after our daughter was born. He didn't tell me he was considering it. He just stopped one day, and never mentioned it again.

REVALUATION (PART III)

So the lion cannot create new values, but it can *create the freedom for new creation* . . . And if one can manage to move beyond establishing the preconditions then there is the task itself – the task of revaluation. Nietzsche refers to this task as if it is alive, an active, exacting presence: 'the task itself,' he writes, 'has another will – it calls for him to *create values*.' In some of his work, this revaluation of all values is a broad social project. I have to admit to being utterly uninterested in the philosopher-artist's duty to create new values as lawgiving, as civic duty. I am more interested in Nietzsche's sly, seductive address to the individual reader, the one that implores a personal revaluation of values. In other books, Nietzsche disowns the idea of a society-wide revolution. 'For it is selfish to consider one's own judgement a universal law, and this selfishness is blind, petty, and simple because it shows that you haven't yet discovered yourself or created for yourself an ideal of your very own – for this could never be someone else's, let alone everyone's, everyone's!' he explodes.

'Let us therefore *limit* ourselves to the purification of our opinions and value judgements and to the *creation of tables of what is good that are new and all our own*,' he continues. Sure, I think, if I can get past the allure of the lion, the desire to pursue the preconditions forever . . .

MEANING

My son is sitting on the floor to zip up his winter boots. He stops mid-zip and peers up at me. 'Do I have a great dad?' he asks. This is his last task to do before we leave for school and it is raining and I have not had breakfast. My daughter is at her desk making a pile of pens and pencils. ('Look, Maman, I'm going to draw a picture all in different shades of red! What do you think of these shades of red, Maman? Which one should I start with? This is a good idea, isn't it, Maman? To draw a picture like this? I'll start with this colour.') I pause in my search for the keys to peer back at my son before answering, 'I think you may have the *best* Dad.' 'No,' he clarifies, still paused in his task. 'Like "great uncle."' 'Zip. Up. Those. Boots!' I find the keys at the bottom of the bowl. 'No. A "great dad" would be your grandfather, like a great uncle is your parent's uncle.' My throat is hoarse. I grab a scarf from the hook on the back of the door and wind it around my neck. 'No, but like, Uncle Paul, funny Paul, you know, he is my great uncle, he is not my grandfather,' he says, carefully finishing his boots. 'Yes, but he is your great uncle because he is my uncle. Okay, let's go,' I say, and I begin to wave my daughter up and away from her desk towards the door. My son has stood up but has a look of hurt perplexity that I recognise as frustration at being misunderstood. 'But *Uncle Paul* . . .' he begins earnestly, and my daughter interrupts as she breezes past. 'He means stepfather, Maman. He wants to know if he has a stepfather.'

*

In French, *he means* is 'il veut dire', and those words directly translate as *he wants to say*. What impresses me is not my daughter's accuracy, but her *assurance*. She is right, of course. He does mean stepfather.

OTHER WAYS TO LEAVE (DEPARTURE PART V)

There is another way to leave: by plane. After the road north, this is my favourite. It feels the most extreme, the most violent of unstrippings. It feels like erasure. Heading north is a journey inward, into a place both ancient and familiar, but leaving by plane is a stratospheric amputation, a glorious severance, catapulting you into the breathless enormity of elsewhere. Leaving by plane is like taking off a suit made of rocks and diving naked into a glacial lake. It is terrifying, invigorating, confusing. It is harder to leave this way. More expensive, more final, more addictive.

MEANING (PART II)

Chapter IV of *The Elements of Style* lists the word *meaningful* as a 'bankrupt adjective.' 'Choose another, or rephrase,' the authors counsel.

SCORN (PART II)

My scorn at my nihilism professor was hasty. When is it not? After I left Paris, I slipped back into the world of obligation and economic responsibility and I didn't choose art – not even close. I had my babies. I became a teacher. I forgot about making – about my own creative impulses. About the darkness. And it came for me. It came for me the way things do, when you ignore them for too long, when you try to make them submit to reason and order. The way Dionysus comes for Pentheus. Came like a monster with a cavernous mouth, an insatiable appetite. Tore me limb from limb. Swallowed me up. Left me to stew in its digestive juices before it shat me out as something else, something deformed, something new. It sent me back, in a black mood, to my notebooks, back to Nietzsche and that moment of pure scorn at my professor who had not realised that a very valid, very credible, very sane response to pure nihilism and apocalyptic sentiment was poetry, love, connection, family.

Libraries (Part III)

'People often say that a set of books looks ugly if all volumes are not in the same format, but I was impressed to hear the Abbot Kōyū say, "It is typical of the unintelligent man to insist on assembling complete sets of everything. Imperfect sets are better." In everything, no matter what it may be, uniformity is undesirable. Leaving something incomplete makes it interesting and gives one the feeling that there is room for growth.' Yoshida Kenkō on the value of the imperfect again.

Research (Part VII)

Many of Nietzsche's books are fragmentary, haphazard, contradictory, ecstatic, defiant, satirical, exasperating and breathtakingly ambitious. His work is subjective, reflective, bombastic, earnest and impressively quotable, resonant, topical. My crocodile-skin shod and crushed-velvet-suited professor called Nietzsche's work 'a vampiric system', in that it sucks you in. 'Nietzsche belongs,' he said, 'to the province of the adolescent.' I suppose because many of us associate adolescence with the longing for vampiric systems to be sucked in by. Especially those that romanticise violent upheaval, that advocate for destruction in the name of creation, that admonish us to unshackle ourselves, to joyfully renounce our duties to everyone and everything but ourselves, and to prioritise our own becoming.

Nobody ever says 'Nietzsche belongs to the province of the middle-aged parent.'

'To see him as a poet is to miss his philosophical value, to see him as a philosopher is to ignore his impetuous poetics,' I have copied down in my lectures notes in yet another one of my notebooks.

PETITE VALISE

I am in bed; I cannot seem to be able to get up. My daughter makes me a little cardboard suitcase – she writes 'Valise Petite' on the front, meaning 'Little Suitcase', and fills it with objects she has made out of paper and masking tape – a phone, an orange, a sandwich, a pen and a pencil, a small booklight and two books. One book is called *The Book of the Good* and the other is *The Book of the Bad*. Each book is filled with portraits – the good portraits smiling, surrounded by wavy lines that look like wind, the bad portraits grinning, scowling, wielding swords, waist deep in waves.

SCORN (PART III)

It is cheerfully obvious to me now, looking back through my note-books, why my professor was so scornful and dismissive of my choice to be a mother and a poet. It's right there in lecture four, and in all his Marxist allusions – his contempt for the bodily imperative in the modern state to be of economic value by *producing* and *creating*. It's in Nietzsche too, in his scorn for women, for their preoccupation with *aut liberi aut libri* – 'either children or books', the life of the family or life of the mind. Choosing to drop out and make babies and write poems must have seemed like a complete refusal of everything he had taught us – an embrace of the mediocre, the banal, the suburban. I was not putting up any resistance to the ongoing economic obligation to *produce* and *create*. He did not understand that I was interested in what might be built on top of the rubble left in the wake of these theories of destruction; I was not able, then, to explain it.

DEPARTURE (PART VI)

My last fleeing, shedding, glorious, one-way-ticket departure, had been characteristically opportunistic. I was in a meeting when my boss began to talk about the possibility of secondment to a university in Japan. I started texting Guillaume under the table: *Wanna move to Japan?* I wrote, and *Yes*, he replied immediately. And so we did. I was offered the job and accommodation on campus, and Guillaume sidestepped effortlessly from a job in community radio to a PhD on Japanese cinema zombies. 'Zombies?' people would ask, baffled. 'Your PhD is on zombies?' I saw that move to Japan as an opportunity to be reinvented, to be stripped back, to be rewired, to experience yet again the thrilling renunciation and razing that I had become addicted to, that I associated with growth and development. Except, of course, I was not going alone. I was going with a spouse, a three-year-old, a five-year-old, and four suitcases filled mostly with Lego.

PARIS (PART V)

My nihilism course ended with Zygmunt Bauman. My notes from that class are particularly careful – I had been tasked with keeping notes for my friend Alex, who was absent that day. I made my closest friends in that course: international students like me, multilingual loners and losers obsessed with theory in a gorgeous, foreign metropolis that did not care about us. The notes are funny – a long section about our modern lack of solid relationships and the bonds that have been frayed by liquid modernity is peppered with marginalia and asides for my friend's benefit, noting that Bauman's observations do not apply to us. 'The horror of inadequacy replaces the horror of conformity – we are always lacking', I have written, with the addition, 'but not us, babe – we're not lacking.'

Sometimes I like to imagine the course I'd teach if I were a lecturer at my old university in Paris. I'd call it 'Reparation, Revaluation and Procreation: Sticking with the Trouble and Art after The End.' The reading list would feature Eve Sedgwick and Olivia Laing and Maggie Nelson and Virginia Woolf and Ursula le Guin and Sei Shōnagon and Elena Ferrante and Anne Carson and Ryszard Kapuscinski, what Olivia Laing calls 'work that bubbles with generosity, amusement, innovation and creative rage'. We'd spend the semester attempting to engage with a humanist feminist's inexplicable appetite for philosophies of despair. It would be a course that was based on hunting around in the darkness for poetic joy, for creative rage, for an emboldened and emboldening art that is making a play for meaning, for value, in a world that wants us to remain mindless consumers obsessed with the contemporary apocalypse.

SMOKING (PART II)

Although I have no clear memory of actively quitting smoking, I do remember my final cigarette, because it was many years after I had stopped. Guillaume and I were living in Hanoi, my most favourite of cities. The night of my last cigarette, I was knocked over by a motorbike full of boys who were swerving dangerously through the traffic as I was crossing the street. I crumpled to the ground as if I were made of paper; they screeched off, barely registering the impact, while I struggled to crawl to the other side of the road, away from the nighttime river of bikes and the risk of being hit again. I remember it as being an incredible rush, both horrible and joyful, a feeling of being knocked clean out of myself, of having my breath suddenly depart, a feeling almost beautiful in the sincerity and suddenness of impact.

Guillaume literally dusted me off, patting down my faux-leather jacket with pink leopard print lining that I'd bought the day before. 'I want a gin and a smoke,' I said, shaking, and he didn't resist, steering me quickly into the sanctuary of the upstairs bar we were headed for. He handed me the cigarette, skinny and brown, like I remembered them, and I took a deep drag before screwing up my face in revulsion. 'That's fucking disgusting,' I said, and he laughed. 'Why did you want one?' he asked. 'I think I wanted something that no longer exists,' I exhaled. 'What a cigarette used to be, when I used to want them.'

NIHILISM (PART III)

These days I am tempted to define nihilism as a mood, rather than trying to deconstruct it, or determine an exact meaning. I'm less interested in all the historical, political, philosophical, and poetical costumes it has worn over the centuries. Posturing atheist, challenger, liberator, ruinous madman. Apocalyptic saviour. Vitriolic insult. Solitary hope. I have this feeling that if I can carry it into my research as a mood, rather than a concept, I can look for it in a sensory way, rather than a cerebral one. I can slip into the texts and sniff around, listening carefully and running my hands along the walls of words, digging into the earth of the narrative and unpegging the language from the line of reasoning.

AILLEURS (ELSEWHERE)

Perhaps because of the stories I grew up with, or perhaps because of the people who told them, I have never felt at ease at home. I always have an eye on the horizon, a sense of biding my time, of putting up resistance to the magnetic pull of the faraway. As an adult I have given in to the drag of it many times, letting myself get swept back from the shore of the known into the waters of obscurity and disorientation. Leaving creates a silence that is hypnotic, the sudden quiet of either cure or relapse, depending on perspective.

> Maybe because we know we can never correct the absence that defines our shared past, that pictures and money don't ease the fact of such absence – maybe that's why we keep leaving. Why I keep leaving.
>
> – Beth Nguyen, 'Apparent'

Going and
Not Going

All this about staying where you are, dying, living, being born, unable to go forward or back, not knowing where you came from, or where you are, or where you're going, or that it's possible to be elsewhere, to be otherwise, supposing nothing, asking yourself nothing, you can't, you're there, you don't know who, you don't know where.

– Samuel Beckett, *The Unnamable*

LOCKED

Locked, then. The ongoing border restrictions mean that escape is snatched from us, and when it becomes clear there is no timeline for re-opening, it's like waking from a dream – the shock of returning to a landlocked body, suddenly only a part of *this* topography and *this* time zone. As if we had been living in a dozen different dimensions, slipping between states, only to wake to find the wormholes cauterised. The skies become blank and blue as I have rarely seen them, quiet and expansive without the chalky criss-cross of contrails. Now we are exclusively local, forced to confront our native state. But the foreign – being foreign, becoming foreign – wasn't that always a delusion? Wasn't *elsewhere* the delusion?

Howling

My self-care is not working, I text a friend. *I need to up my game.* She replies with a screengrab from Instagram. *Self-care is over*, it says. *Now we are taking acid and howling at the moon.*

Aphorism

The problem with self-care, of course, is that it's just *another type of care*.

Deficit

I run long distances in silence. I eat tuna out of a can instead of making lunch. I stare into the distance and do not respond when people ask what I am thinking. I take naps at 2pm. I read Nietzsche in the sun. A doctor has prescribed Vitamin D supplements to me and every other woman I know. FOR LIFE, one doctor wrote on a friend's prescription, underlining it twice. Why are we all so fucking deficient? What are we getting wrong?

In *The Antichrist*, Nietzsche argues that 'Christianity needs sickness almost as much as Hellenism needs a superfluity of health.' I could have a superfluity of health, I think. Enough with this pasty, feeble flesh! I have two goals for the summer: to get an even tan, and to read all of Beckett. I have a stack of books and five bikinis. Everything else is an act of cowardice, or terrorism. Most of the time: both.

DOMESTIC

I begin to resent disruption. I no longer like to work in snatches – I feel rushed, robbed, irritable. Suddenly, my children are furiously joyful noise-machines, a violence against any act of making. 'The problem,' my husband muses one morning, 'is that they are just too happy.'

DISJECTA MEMBRA

All that Donatello left behind in that city [Siena], in the Office of Works of the Duomo, was a bronze figure of St John the Baptist, with its right arm missing below the elbow; and this, it is said, was because he had not been fully paid for it.

– Giorgio Vasari, *Lives of the Artists (vol. 1)*

IMAGINE

Imagine a woman raised in the spirit of leaving, genetically wired to flee, who married the wildest, most solitary man she had ever met – imagine how they might have ranged out, burning up past lives like so many combustible bridges. Imagine how reckless they might have been; imagine the plans they might have had.

DOMESTIC (PART II)

We have an argument one night over dinner. The children are talking too much and not eating. I have made them nachos and I am suddenly exhausted in the face of children who talk too much to eat their goddamn nachos. 'It is very easy to make me happy,' I snap. 'All I want is for you to be polite, and grateful, and to eat your dinner.' 'I thought you *also* wanted us to listen to you,' my eight-year-old counters. 'That falls under the umbrella of "polite",' I reply. 'Huh,' she says thoughtfully. 'I thought things fell on TOP of umbrellas.'

ABSENCE

I begin to lose words. 'Let's turn the page,' I say to my son in a stationery store. He snorts with laughter. 'Do you mean go to the next aisle?' I nod absently. I start to replace nouns with sounds – 'Where's the flippy?' I ask my daughter. I mix up my words – 'Get ready for the kitchen,' I tell them. 'Put on your toothbrushes.' They find this endlessly hilarious. I struggle to name this operational deficiency. Let's call it *presence* for the sake of communicability.

My children regularly recall me from my thoughts because what comes out of my mouth no longer makes sense. 'No, the sunface, that's the one,' I say, as the children roll around with laughter. 'Papa, Maman wants us to use the *sunface*,' they roar. It takes me a few moments to register that they are laughing at me, to remember what I was saying (and why), to decipher what I might have meant. I am slow, it is so slow. 'Why did I say that?' I ask, and my daughter will tell me. 'You want us to use this sunscreen,' she explains kindly. Their questions have become increasingly challenging – either because they are growing older and more complex, or because I am so absent, so completely unable to focus.

In truth, I am not even thinking about something else – my mind is like an ocean that just wants to lap, lap, lap against the shore, and maybe drift in the memory of a previous life, one before the borders closed, when I was swimming out to visit a shrine on a tiny island off the coast, holding a small crustacean in my hands as the waves sparkled in the hot sun.

Interruptions

'Maman, what would it feel like to be nothing?'

Poem

I scrap out a quick poem sitting on the toilet one morning and leave my pen behind on a stack of French parenting magazines. Later I find that one of my children has used the pen to underline seemingly random words in one of the magazines. I flick through the pages, marvelling at the endeavour: two or three words are underlined on each page, some from headlines, others from articles, some even in the small print at the bottom of full-page advertisements. Some words are just underlined with a wobbly blue dash, others are harshly underscored. I take the magazine to my desk and press it flat, typing out the words in order:

> dans parents sérieusement triste qui restera que maîtresse perçoit à fonde Maman confinement intellectuel chauffer séparation une enfant Maman ne d'être projection faire classe que origines opus seul de résister décalé comptines dinosaure humains soit famille veut par posés sportifs

As I translate, I shift a few of the word forms around and ensure that the conjugations agree, and a poem emerges:

In seriously sad parents / who will only remain teachers / we can perceive that at heart, Maman, intellectually confined, will separate, via heat, from her child / Maman: not a projection / made only of her class origins / containing an opus / must be solitary. / To resist the quirky nursery rhymes / the human dinosaurs / *to be family* / requires an athletic response.

'Maman, intellectually confined, will separate, via heat, from her child.'

EXPECTATION

I chat to my neighbour over the brush fence. I can almost feel the ghost of a cigarette and a floral apron, as if this were the 1950s and I had six children. I am telling her about the chicken paella I am making, and she is explaining her keto diet. We watch the children skateboarding in the cul-de-sac. The next morning, she slows her car to lean out the window and ask me, in a bright, friendly voice, 'How was dinner?' 'It was disgusting,' I reply. 'I had to chuck it in the bin.' She stares at me blankly, and then says: 'That is not what I expected you to say,' before driving off.

I am filled with a sudden and frightful glee. I cannot do things, I am making rubbish. A bit like this. What I am trying to make. Sudden and unexpected shit. *Quelle misère.*

*

Great talents encourage great incapacities, but maintaining an inability to cook an egg or drive a car won't make you into a genius.

– Sarah Manguso, *300 Arguments*

(*But won't it?* a part of me whispers.)

Bullshit

My favourite French expression is *n'importe quoi*, translated variously as 'whatever' or 'what nonsense'; sometimes rendered in subtitles as *bullshit*. Whenever I say it to the children they shriek with laughter – so unexpected it is for me to round on them in French for whatever absurdity they are trying to tell me, to convince me is real. My personal translation for *n'importe quoi* is 'humbug'. It doesn't have the same feel in the mouth, on the tongue, but if my mother had said 'humbug' to me as a child, I too would have hooted with delight.

Parameters

We have clear parameters to our movements – to minimise contagion, we must not cross state lines. The border elbows out into hard corners at the top and sprawls out as raggedy coastline below. Mapped edges that once delineated a silhouette to be printed on tourism material now rear up at us like walls of stone. We are surrounded by an uncrossable moat. We buy lanterns and sleeping bags and a camp-stove. Cut off like this, we commit ourselves to a different kind of adventure, a sort of moonshine *ailleurs*, 'elsewhere'.

SILENCE

My children are suspicious of silence. If I am silent, something is wrong. We are not a naturally quiet family. They do not like me to be silent. They like me to chatter, to laugh, to respond, to engage. I have to explain if I want to be quiet, if I want them to be quiet. I am tired, I have a headache. I often want to be quiet. I often ask them to talk to each other, instead of to me. I tell them I cannot multitask; I cannot talk while making breakfast, eating breakfast, reversing the car, driving the car, folding clothes, measuring flour, running a bath, or thinking.

SOBRIETY

I begin to think about addiction and escape. I stop drinking entirely in some inexplicable pact with Nietzsche – something about being committed to being with, or in, the grief of life. Relentlessly working at the coalface of lack, without lubricating or looking away. Nietzsche had a lot to say about alcohol, about its numbing, dumbing effects. In *Ecce Homo* Nietzsche includes sobriety as one of the reasons why he is so clever. 'Alcohol is bad for me,' Walter Kaufmann translates, 'a single glass of wine or beer in one day is quite sufficient to turn my life into a vale of misery . . . [I] cannot advise all *more spiritual* natures earnestly enough to abstain entirely from alcohol. *Water* is sufficient.' Nietzsche is also against coffee, declaring that it 'spreads darkness'. Besides alcohol and coffee, Nietzsche famously had a lot of negative things to say about women, about the English, about his fellow Germans. Some things I discard, derisively, some things I polish, some things I put in my pocket for later.

*

Not drinking is not hard, but it is awkward. Drinkers are sloppy, and women like me (read: intense, drowning, wilful) are meant to drink to defer the pain of mothering, to stake a claim to their rock'n'roll past, as part of a performance of fuck-it hedonism. Not drinking delineates me as puritanical, joyless, exhausting. Combined with my absence from social media I am basically Amish. I haven't learned to say *I don't drink* in a way that doesn't make me sound like an alcoholic. I rehearse sometimes in my head – *It's not for me*; *Not at the moment*; *It's not my thing*. 'You don't drink?' a man asks me carefully on New Year's Eve, after I clumsily refuse his offer of a drink. 'She's on a philosophical quest,' my husband explains helpfully.

NOSTALGIA

In the middle of this summer of tanning and reading Nietzsche and Beckett and howling at the moon I begin to wake rotten with longing for far-away places and long-ago lives. I figure it to be a hangover from my dreams, places that I visit in my sleep. I dream most often of our life in Japan. The sprawling train station in Hirakata. Charlie's across the road where the bartender would make you a cocktail based on your mood. The yakitori place a few blocks down, full of smoke and huge mugs of beer. The public swimming pool, eerily suspended on the second floor of a building that looked like a glass cruise liner. The bridge over the slow, wide river that filled to roaring with winter rains. The view of the distant theme park in the evenings, lit up like a fairytale. Hot bean cakes and the playground at the top of the hill, the swings that made you feel as though you were flying over the city, cherry blossoms drifting through the air like spring snow.

This rotten longing makes me feel like a failure at living in the moment, at being present with my children, at appreciating my good fortune. Sullen, sulky. *Je ne veux pas être ici.* I don't want to be here, arguing with my son about his breakfast, preparing for a camping trip in the wilderness of the peninsula to the north. I do not want to drive away from the city again, loaded up with plates and sausages and pillows and first aid kits. I want to stay home and write about Hirakata and the river to the east that I walked along when it was raining, past the fragrant camellia and the abandoned Turkish restaurant.

Life is a thing of beauty and a joy forever, I think one morning in the shower. *A thing of beauty and a joy forever.* Through gritted teeth I feel I am saying it, beauty, joy forever. Life. I think of one of Beckett's characters hearing this line, and expressing doubt as to whether it applies to *human* life.

MOUNTAINTOP

Nietzsche is everywhere; don't tell me he isn't. The girls in *White Lotus* are reading him by the pool of their exclusive Hawaiian resort. Eddie Murphy quotes him in *Coming to America*. The French television show *Réunions* starts with a quote from Nietzsche – the one about suffering making you stronger – and then concludes, *mais Nietzsche était un putain de loser!* But Nietzsche was a fucking loser!

One Sunday afternoon on Radio National the philosopher Simon Critchley is discussing Nietzsche and nihilism. 'Do you read Nietzsche when he's writing about this task of creating one's own values and proceeding through pain and self-laceration and coming out the other side, do you read that and think, well, yes, this is for me?' the interviewer asks. 'To be perfectly honest, yes,' Critchley replies. 'He speaks to me like no other philosopher . . . with the qualification that I want my Nietzsche with a kind of side salad of Samuel Beckett. So a Nietzsche with more of a sense of a humour, Nietzsche with more of a sense of decay and decline. What I don't like about Nietzsche is the Nietzsche on the mountaintop, 6,000 feet above man and time, declaiming.'

Personally, I like Nietzsche on the mountaintop, declaiming. But the highest point in the state is a mountain in the remote outback: at 1,435 metres it is hardly the Swiss Alps. And how can you 'be ready to burn yourself in your own flame' when you are a mother and teacher and spouse – in short, when so many people rely on your *stability* and *sameness*?

Beckett as a side salad! I can't stop laughing about this.

Nostalgia (Part II)

I find myself increasingly haunted by intrusive memories of life elsewhere – all of my *ailleurs*. I call the memories intrusive because they blossom in my mind out of nowhere and derail all other thoughts. If my children are at home I will badger them with questions:

Do you remember the place we stayed in Tokyo? It was a hostel, with a big kitchen downstairs? We went for a walk to the museum – that museum, remember? We waited to go in and barely got to see any of it . . . And on the way back, crossing the bridge, we stopped at that speciality bakery, they made some sort of doughnut that we wanted to try, only I can't remember exactly . . . And I couldn't wait any longer, I was too hot and tired, and I went back to the room before you . . .

Most of them are like this – memories I think of as *thwarted memories*. The times I went searching for art or adventure and only got a glimpse of what I was seeking. I had to learn the art of pocketing what I could. Perhaps that is why these memories persist, because I stored them away in memory-velvet, as if each one was an heirloom. When we visited Byōdō-in, the Buddhist temple in Uji, I pocketed the sight of the heron standing delicately in the water before the great Phoenix Hall, the statue of Murasaki Shikibu by the river, the cascading wisteria in front of the temple. I thought to myself, *I will come back*, and that comforted me as I was rushed through the temple, as I had to find toilets and lunch for the children, as I had to answer dozens and dozens of questions.

But of course I never did return. There was too little time, too many other places to visit. The only returning I can do now is like this, as a daydream, *en rêve*.

LUSTSPIEL

'Tonight I take it out to the porch and miss you, one word at a time. *Lustspiel*, I slowly mouth into the dark blue night,' writes Sabrina Orah Mark in *The Babies*. The fragment is titled 'Box Three, Spool Five' in reference to Beckett's *Krapp's Last Tape*. I read this in a tent with no mobile reception or dictionary, and I have to guess what lustspiel means. Is it an invented word? Because of the title, I think of a *spiel* as being something that unravels from a spool. I imagine my longing being spun out of my chest into a thread that can be wound around a spool in the dark of the campground, ready for me to carry it home.

When we get back in range, I look it up – the word *lustspiel* is German; it means 'comedy'. *Spiel* means game. It has nothing to do with the spool of longing that is now stored carefully at the bottom of my backpack, waiting to see what I will make of it.

CAMPING

Before one of our trips, I give my daughter the whittling knife she has been begging for. She cuts herself twice. The first time I gasp in fright and she bursts into tears. The second time I scold her for not showing me earlier, and I scrub the cut with an alcohol wipe I fish out of the first aid kit. If she cuts herself a third time, she does not tell me about it.

One of the campsites we stay at is full of harried mothers who keep screeching at sons who all have the same names as my ex-boyfriends. The sons are insolent; the sons are confused. 'Tom! Tom! Stop . . . give me *that!* I told you not to touch – LOOK AT WHAT YOU'VE – I *cannot* – CANNOT – RYAN! WHAT ARE YOU *doing* you're going to – it's going to – !' The mothers are exhausted; the mothers are demented. What interests me most is the fathers and husbands, skinny and swarthy, like marathon runners. After long hikes, they return in the evenings in silence, looking a decade younger than their wives.

NIETZSCHE AS SOFTWARE

Critchley says that in the late 1980s the French-Algerian philosopher Jacques Derrida described Nietzsche's philosophy as a sort of software technology, back when metaphors about computers and computer processing were relatively new. Derrida posited that Nietzsche's philosophy was a kind of unstable program that had different applications – that could be thrown into culture and have weird and unexpected effects, effects Nietzsche never intended. Nietzsche's work can be – and has been – appropriated for a plethora of agendas in the last hundred years; artistic, literary, poetic, philosophical, political.

For a while I wonder if this fact that he is so easily appropriated, so easily instrumentalised, explains why I carry Nietzsche with me everywhere as we range out over the state, tucking *Beyond Good and Evil* into my backpack and, at one point, fanning a campfire into life with *The Antichrist* (literally *fanning the flames with Nietzsche*). But Nietzsche's software stops working after a while – he wants me to flee and I cannot. Where am I if I am not fleeing? Who am I? I am waiting, suspended. I am going, but not going. Stuck in a loop. Steppenwolf pacing back and forth in an enclosure. *A thing of beauty and a joy forever.*

Questions (Part II)

Where does a humanitarian nihilist turn when she cannot (motherhood, wifehood, pandemic lockdown) raze it all and start again?

The Wreck of the Hesperus

On the last night of one of our camping trips, we eat at a restaurant near the campsite. It is a sticky, dusty evening, and mosquitoes are butting against the window near our table. I feel bone tired; the meal is mediocre, and after the children order dessert ('Should I get sprinkles, Maman? Sprinkles are more fun. But do you think I will like them? Do they make it taste worse? Or better? Or neither? Maybe I'll get them. They are more fun') I go to the bathroom and sit on the toilet seat for fifteen minutes in total silence, except for the woman in the cubicle next to me who speaks to herself, twice. The first time she mutters, 'Oh, just shut up,' and I turn towards her voice as if I can see through the walls of the cubicle. Then, at the mirror, she sighs loudly and says: 'I look like the wreck of the *Hesperus*.' I try to get a look at her through the gap in the toilet door, but all I see is a flutter of grey-blue, the same colour as the hemp-denim shirt dress I am wearing.

In the restaurant I scan for her discreetly, but it seems that all the women here are wearing some variation on grey-blue. None of them look specifically like the wreck of the *Hesperus*. All of them look as if they might, in a secret moment, turn to the mirror and say that they do.

NOSTALGIA (PART III)

I cannot remember the name of the museum we visited in Tokyo, the one we got through four rooms of before the children were hungry and misbehaving and bored. I have multiple webpages open as I trawl through maps and image searches and try to remember the name of the major exhibitions, but I am distracted by memories and inclined to give up.

I make a coffee and ask my husband about it – he remembers, too, the way we slumped, miserably, into our seats at the museum café and gazed at each other as the children pawed through the menu. By this stage our daughter could read and speak Japanese better than we could, and she was translating menu items for us with glee. 'I'm going back to look at the gift shop,' I muttered, and Guillaume nodded wearily. At the gift shop I flicked through commodified versions of artworks I would never see and bought a square pocket handkerchief of a print I did not recognise; bracken and wildflowers inked in sage and charcoal.

As soon as I remember this handkerchief I get down on my hands and knees and pull a bag of scarves out from under the bed. There it is – TOKYO NATIONAL MUSEUM printed carefully in the bottom right corner.

I think I am shit at research because I no longer believe in anything out there, beyond us – anything the internet tells me exists, anything a map might reveal. The only faith I have is in pulling carefully at the thread of memory until it leads to something here in front of me. A scrap of fabric I hold in my hands.

Domestic (Part III)

I have often felt myself to be the human parent of animals. Barbaric, furious, irrational, creative, vivacious animals. Sometimes I like it, like when they howl in anger at getting a splinter or spend an hour talking to a millipede. Other times I crack under the strain of it, snapping at my children to stop drinking their milk like cats. 'Why would you get a pet?' I growl at my husband. 'It would be like having a toddler that will never grow up.'

Sobriety (Part II)

Sobriety is a bit like lockdown. It is the sudden elimination of an escape route – not a blockage, but an erasure. Once we were torrential rains pouring down a mountainside, channelling in any direction that suited us, and now we are contained in a glass, a tall skinny receptacle that we must learn to live inside, clinking together like cubes of ice. I wonder about the links between nihilism and escapism, about pleasure and purpose. About denial and creation. About refusal and joy.

My refusal to drink is a performance, an intentional restriction. It's a scowling rejection of the hungover, seedy carelessness that I have always found seductive. *I give you up I give you up I give you up*, I mutter to myself, trying to commit to this dead philosopher and his mad rants and the teeth-scraping pain of life.

Olivia Laing's *The Trip to Echo Spring: On Writers and Drinking* is about alcoholic writers – six in particular, all men, all Americans. Carver, Cheever, Hemingway, F. Scott Fitzgerald, Tennessee Williams, and John Berryman. In a later article, Laing confides that the question she is asked most about this book is *What about women?* In response, she describes the 'brilliant, restless figures' of Jean Rhys and Marguerite Duras, whose works reflect the violence and degradation of their lives, and the 'savage, haunted account[s] of stacked cards and loaded dice that might drive even the sanest woman to drink and drink and drink'.

NOSTALGIA (PART IV)

Suffering makes the imagination weak and lazy; it moves, but unwillingly and heavily, with the weak movements of someone who is ill, with the weariness and caution of sick, feverish limbs; it is difficult for us to turn our eyes away from our own life and our own state, from the thirst and restlessness that pervade us. And so memories of our own past constantly crop up in the things we write, our own voice constantly echoes there and we are unable to silence it.

– Natalia Ginzburg, 'My Vocation', *The Little Virtues*

Necessity

Because of my project, people begin to recommend fragmentary narratives to me. Many of these books grapple with the pressures of parenting young children, and the pressure this role places on artists. Kate Zambreno describes fragmentation as a creative choice:

> There's this marvelous moment in Rivka Galchen's *Little Labors* . . . where the narrator reflects that after having a child she is full of more rich thinking than ever, but the thoughts pass by, she has less time to write them down. Which allows for this fragmented form.

I am struck by this use of the word 'allows' – I could never be that gracious. I am inclined to say 'necessitates': I find myself closer in sympathy to Raymond Carver's description of the pressure having small children put on his creative output:

> During these ferocious years of parenting, I usually didn't have the time, or the heart, to think about working on anything very lengthy. The circumstances of my life, the 'grip and slog' of it, in D.H. Lawrence's phrase, did not permit it . . . Looking back on it now, I think I was slowly going nuts with frustration during those ravenous years. Anyway, these circumstances dictated, to the fullest possible extent, the forms my writing could take.

Slowly going nuts, I nod slowly. *Ravenous years.*

WHAT WORKING DOES TO THE TROUBLE

I was in fact as sick as I have ever been when I was writing 'Slouching Towards Bethlehem'; the pain kept me awake at night and so for twenty and twenty-one hours a day I drank gin-and-hot-water to blunt the pain and took Dexedrine to blunt the gin and wrote the piece. (I would like you to believe that I kept working out of some real professionalism, to meet the deadline, but that would not be entirely true; I did have a deadline, but it was also a troubled time, and working did to the trouble what gin did to the pain.)

– Joan Didion, Preface to *Slouching Towards Bethlehem*

Nietzsche, like Didion, was also forced to work against debilitating episodes of pain, and illness. Both suffered from migraines; both had to spend long periods of time in bed. Nietzsche also had bad eyesight and fits of vomiting. His letters and diaries and notebooks record his ongoing battle with illness. Although I know Nietzsche's famously aphoristic style was developed partly in response to the limited amount of time he could spend writing, I am still surprised by how many modern fragmentary narratives I encounter lean into decline, trauma, and impairment – 'drifting into the arena of the unwell' as the narrator in *Withnail and I* puts it. I am determined to resist this drift. This is partly an artistic choice, partly constitutional. I cannot, however much I try, maintain the necessary space between myself and these narratives. I read illness with my body, caving inwards with each trauma, shuddering with shock. So much *blood*. I finally give up, unable to 'read' with the proper distance, returning the books to the shelf.

SEDUCTION

I begin to think that all writing is an act of seduction and all reading an act of being seduced. Nietzsche is good at this, good at seduction. *Écriture séduisante.* 'Nietzsche writes exclusively for you. Not at you, but for you. For you, the reader. Only you,' writes David B. Allison. I love this about his work – the intimate address, his defiant sense of form, his insistence on expressing his ideas in an artistic and elegant way. 'Perhaps it is nothing but an urge, an aspiration, a clumsy access of admiration, a *crush*,' Brian Dillon speculates about loving a writer's style. '"I like your style" means: I admire, dear human, what you have clawed back from sickness and pain and madness. I'm a fan, too much a fan, of your *rising above*.'

SOLITUDE

We are born, sworn, jealous friends of solitude, our own deepest, most midnightly, noon-likely solitude. This is the type of people we are, we free spirits! and perhaps you are something of this yourselves, you who are approaching? you new philosophers?

– Friedrich Nietzsche, *Beyond Good and Evil*

I know I need to move on from Nietzsche, even as I struggle to locate a way out from under his shadow. The camel in me is heavy with the weight of his words, the lion is beginning to bristle. 'The complete woman perpetrates literature in the same way she perpetrates a little sin: as an experiment, in passing, looking around to see if someone notices and so that someone may notice . . .' I find myself measuring my life against quotes like this and gritting my teeth. What about all the *complete women* who are desperate to go unnoticed, who wish for more anonymity, who are tired of being the epicentre and

the weathervane of their families' moods? I am a disappointment –
Nietzsche wants me to be full of the rage and fury of adolescence,
of shimmering potential, an uncompromising warrior. But I am not
an adolescent: I am a mother in the middle of a pandemic, I lack
the space and the silence to make what I want to make. My *lustspiel*
remains wound tight.

THE UNTIMELY

Irving Goh, writing about Nietzsche, claims that the space to 'stand
apart from the rest of the world', in the form of rejection of what is
popular or trending or contemporary, is to be protected because it
offers a valuable space from which we can critique the world. Nietzsche
regularly refers to this as the *untimely*. Sue Prideaux, in her riotous
biography *I am Dynamite!*, describes the period of Nietzsche's life
in which he was planning his *Untimely Meditations* series. '*Untimely*
is a small and overlooked work in English,' she explains, 'but for
Nietzsche *unzeitgemässe* was a word of great stature. It meant standing
outside time forward and time backward: outside current fashion
and outside the drag-anchor of history, too.'

QUESTIONS (PART III)

How to get into the untimely?

NECESSITY (PART II)

A friend once described becoming bored with a book in which a
variety of writers explained their creative practice. 'Literally all the

men are quoted saying things like, "O fickle muse! I live to serve your sweet music." And the women are like, "Yeah, I just get up early."' I laughed in delight when she told me this, but I still experience the nauseating wrongness of having to perpetually bat away the desire to write, to respond to the click of inspiration. What can a mother do in the time after she rises, and what doesn't get made because she cannot write 'when the muse is upon her'? 'We are traditionally rather proud of ourselves,' Toni Morrison tells us, 'for having slipped creative work in there between the domestic chores and obligations. I'm not sure we deserve such big A-pluses for all that.'

DOMESTIC (PART IV)

Sometimes my neighbours fight and freak me out. They're a family of six, living in a house ten times the size of ours. It's the grandparents who fight, screaming hysterically at each other in altercations that last for hours, the kind of arguments that rupture families and poison generations. I hang out the washing and listen, unable to discern the gist of the dispute, inventing stories to make sense of his explosive, emphatic ranting and her shrieking, blustering replies. Sometimes the two are separated by the younger couple and guided to different parts of the house, where presumably only I can hear them, each still screaming abuses about the other. Him in the upstairs corner north window, her by the overgrown herb garden.

Anyone who has watched a parent fall in love only to have that love go terribly wrong, who has witnessed the sleight-of-hand that transforms a slightly cantankerous boyfriend into a man who likes to leave bruises on their mother, who failed for years to extricate a parent from the sticky and too-often deadly web of domestic violence, will recognise the hypervigilance at work here. I feel full body panic sometimes trying to imagine how my mother would have survived the pandemic if she were still with her ex. I try to keep an open mind, I try not to jump to conclusions.

But one night there are police cars, and I recognise the daughter's shame as she tries to explain their presence to the neighbours ('My father sometimes gets very angry'), and it becomes impossible for me to wave at the grandfather as he wheels his granddaughter around on her trike.

DESOLATE

I keep picking up Nietzsche, keep flinging him across the room. I feel like I'm constantly coming across passages like this:

> The literary woman, unsatisfied, agitated, desolate in heart and entrails, listening every minute with painful curiosity to the imperative which whispers from the depths of her organism: *aut liberi aut libri.*

Again with the binary: 'either books, or babies'. I am enraged by this comment, and simultaneously by how difficult it is to parent whilst trying to create, by how 'desolate' I feel in my 'heart and entrails'.

TSUNDOKU

I have stopped reading; I have no time. The books in their unmoving stack judge me as I wipe and clean and cook and calm and kiss and cajole and snap. In Japanese they have a word for this – *tsundoku,* to acquire books with the intention of reading them but instead letting them pile up. The word *tsunde-oku* means to pile things up ready for later and then leave them, and *dokusho* means reading books. I cannot quite work out if I am *tsundoku-ing* or if the piles themselves are *tsundoku*. I could write to my Japanese friends to ask, but I don't.

Voices

Constantly longing to be elsewhere is inconvenient, and so whenever I notice that I have drifted into farsickness, a voice in my head shouts, ÇA N'A RIEN À VOIR AVEC MON FUTUR! *This has nothing to do with my future.* Perhaps *futur* should be *avenir*, perhaps I should say *cela* instead of *ça*. But that is not what the voice in my head shouts – and what does it matter, *how could it possibly matter*. I don't know why the shout is in French. I hear it in my mother-in-law's voice, lilting up on the *rien-à-voir*, telling me off in her bold, brassy tones, full of comedy, full of authority. After the shouting, I try to clear my mind of everything but the royal blue salvia in the garden, the fuchsia crepe myrtles, the geometric euphorbia with its lime green bouquet. I recite them like an obsessive collector: *acacia, melaleuca, callistemon*, trying to anchor myself to the here and now.

Lost and Found

What we lose and what we find in the pandemic is impossible to quantify, even to explain. 'I want a lost and found in my living room,' Sabrina Orah Mark writes, 'manned daily by [Virginia] Woolf. A small booth with a sliding window. Tap, tap. Woolf slides the window open. "State your missing." And I state my missing. Obviously she never returns anything. But just hearing her sort through the missing is a comfort.'

MOTHERING

My children are asked to complete a questionnaire about their home life. One of the tasks asks them to 'Describe your mother in one word'. 'Strict,' my son says, and my daughter replies 'Jolly' at the same time.

AUDIBLE

When we find ourselves unable to return to his homeland indefinitely, Guillaume – who left France as a young man, convinced he did not belong – is rattled. The forceful boundedness of the lockdown shakes him, and he leaks French all over our lives in response. He loads up every speaker with mixes of French music, the floor becomes littered with French comics and in the evenings he is tired and wants to watch French films, French television. *Par contre*, he speaks less and less in French, as if he has cordoned off that part of himself, the verbal, the part that exhales. We only breathe French in, we do not speak it, we do not speak of it. It is as if *ailleurs* is a wound we do not allow ourselves to poke.

VOICES (PART II)

Unable to read, I find myself on a restless binge of Beckett audiobooks instead, narrated by the voice actor Seán Barrett. I burn through *Molloy*, *Malone Dies*, and *The Unnamable* as the summer wears on, filling my head with voices and words as I fold endless piles of laundry. I listen to the books in English. Beckett originally composed them in French, but then translated the works back into English himself, a decision I find both strange and fascinating. I find

70

listening to his writing hypnotic, a joyful surrender. Parts of it make me shout with laughter; I love every time he moans about his awful prose. The characters are always wildly aware of their own decomposition, confusion, inability to hold onto any sense of purpose or belonging. The voices that torment his narrators exist only to serve me; they do not require answers or guidance or instructions. They allow me to do nothing but listen, to be passive, to be silent.

Deficit (Part II)

Another obsession I develop that summer is a black dress I come across online; kimono-sleeves, a fitted pencil-skirt base and an open keyhole back. I revisit the webpage a dozen times a day, filling and emptying the virtual shopping cart with the dress as if my deficit is tangible and I can purchase what I am missing. As if what I am missing is 48% cupro, 30% linen, 22% tencel and made in China.

Seduction (Part II)

I may not know how to seduce but I will dazzle. (Nothing will distract me from pain.) You have to wait. Have to wait for me to renounce (brilliant) rigidity, for me to submit, hidden from my own eyes, to the shadow of desire. Half-way would be enough. The only imperative is that you go on waiting . . .

– María Negroni, *Islandia*

BESOIN

In an essay on art, Beckett described his creative process and what he called *les deux besoins*, the two needs. First, *besoin d'avoir besoin*, and second, *besoin dont on a besoin*. The 'need to have a need', and 'the need one needs'. For a long time I am drawn to trying to understand this essay because of Beckett's insistent and complex repetition of the word *besoin*, 'need'. I feel I am constantly navigating a complex and elusive web of unmet needs, and I want to know why these unmet needs feel so deeply connected to what I am trying, and failing, to write about. I make lists for myself. Need as concave, need as convex. Need as want, need as lack. Need as appetite, need as expulsion. The need for *something*, the need for *nothing*.

But one day I realise the word 'need' is no longer the one I am most preoccupied by: the word that keeps leaping out at me, now, is 'awareness'. Beckett not only details (and diagrams) *les deux besoins*, but also refers to the *conscience de besoin d'avoir besoin*, and the *consciences du besoin dont on a besoin*. These phrases translate roughly as 'the awareness of the need to need', and 'the awareness of the need one needs', or 'the awareness of the need of which we have need'. Whatever my needs are, however opaque, convoluted, impossible, destabilising, maybe even *pointless* – I feel I must now be (need to be) intimately aware of them, must begin to focus exclusively on them, before anything else can happen.

Beckett did not seem to rate this essay of his – in the foreword to the collection he is cited as stating that most of the pieces were written in the spirit of 'friendly obligation or economic need'. The title itself, *Disjecta: Miscellaneous Writings and a Dramatic Fragment*, borrows from the Latin, *disjecta membra*, meaning scattered remains or limbs, but also used to indicate the fragmentary remains of literary or cultural objects, like ancient pottery and verse.

*

Besoin, envie, manque. Need, desire, lack. Sanity, sawn off the shotgun of longing, making it easier to manoeuvre, easier to conceal. How many lives can you miss, in the dark?

INTERRUPTIONS (PART II)

'Maman, I just saw a parrot on a power line in the rain. I'm going to draw that when we get home. Maman, did you hear me, I said I saw a parrot on a line in the rain, and I am going to draw it when I get home. Maman, *can you hear anything I am saying?*'

> At a venture one would say that women's books should be shorter, more concentrated, than those of men, and framed so that they do not need long hours of steady and uninterrupted work. For interruptions there will always be.
>
> – Virginia Woolf, *A Room of One's Own*

COMPOSITION

Beckett began to compose in French after the war, and the humiliating failure of his first two novels. He was living in Paris with his partner, Suzanne Déchevaux-Dumesnil, and while the switch to his second language is not inexplicable, it is unusual. Beckett identified the shift as a creative necessity, intense and urgent. French allowed him to unhook himself from a language that had begun to stifle him. Very few Anglophone writers make the linguistic move away from English. It does, of course, happen. The American writer Jhumpa Lahiri, for example, moved to Rome in 2012 and began composing exclusively in Italian. But writers like Lahiri and Beckett are magical exceptions, drawn to something other than mastery, other than ease.

Beckett's first novel, *Watt*, was composed in English during the war, and is comical in its insistent use of obscure vocabulary and grammatical gymnastics. I am making my way through *Watt* when my daughter comes home to announce that her French teacher will not let her read French novels in class that contain more than three words per page that my daughter does not already know. I narrow my eyes; I consider sending her teacher the handwritten dictionary I have been keeping of the words in *Watt* that I do not know.

primeur – epithalamium – tonsure – tardigrade – funambulistic – ischium – sudarium – pullulate – excoriations – dianoetic – cromlech – scrofulous – eructate – chyle – emoluments – fistular – caecum – exsanguine – lachesis – xenium

Beckett was characteristically vague on his switch to French, describing it as instinctive:

Since 1945 I have written only in French. Why this change? It was not deliberate . . . You may put me in the dismal category of those who, if they had to act in full awareness of what they were doing, would never act. *Which does not preclude there being urgent reasons*, for this change. I myself can half make out several, now that it is too late to go back. But I prefer to let them stay in the half-light. I will all the same give you one clue: *the need to be ill-equipped*.

This claim, in the original French, to have been motivated by 'le besoin d'être mal armé', is considered a play on words: mal armé meaning crippled, or disarmed, 'poorly equipped', could also be an allusion to the poet and critic Stéphane Mallarmé, whom Beckett greatly admired. Beckett found a freedom in being *mal armé*, a limitation that created spaciousness, that helped to clear away the dross of allusion and literary ambition that he felt dogged his attempts to compose in English.

My 'Beckett List' of unfamiliar vocabulary (words to learn before I die) continues, and I begin recording definitions:

velleitary (from the English word 'velleity', meaning merely willing or desiring something without making any effort or taking any action to achieve what one desires) – anhelating (from Latin, meaning aspiring, yearning)

INTERRUPTIONS (PART III)

What's the opposite of Wednesday? my son asks.
Can you eat a tyre? my daughter wants to know.

VEILS

In an essay titled 'The Young Samuel Beckett', J. M. Coetzee describes a letter that Beckett wrote to a young German man named Axel Kaun:

To Kaun he describes language as a veil that the modern writer needs to tear apart if he wants to reach what lies beyond, even if what lies beyond may only be silence and nothingness . . . Though Beckett does not explain to Kaun why French should be a better vehicle than English for the 'literature of the non-word' that he looks forward to, he identifies *'offizielles Englisch'*, formal or cultivated English, as the greatest obstacle to his ambitions.

COMPOSITION (PART II)

When Beckett returned to Paris after the Occupation, biographers report that he and Suzanne were relieved to find their apartment on the rue des Favorites more or less intact. The majority of Beckett's library and papers remained. Enoch Brater suggests that it was at this point Beckett made the deliberate leap into writing in French, rather than his native English, and although finding the library intact and beginning to compose in French are not necessarily related, there is something about this idea of *intactness* that intrigues me. It is the end of the war; Beckett finds his library and papers as he had left them; he begins to compose in his second language of French, the one in which he felt himself necessarily less adroit and therefore, somehow, *uninhibited*. All the material was still there, the weight of the books he had read, the eccentric words he knew – the bookshelves remained, were physically accessible.

The relief of this – the reassurance – seems to me somehow connected to his ability to take the risk – the leap – to work in French. I've been toying with this half idea that Beckett's use of French is a type of linguistic nihilism, via the disintegrating voice, the disintegrating narrative, but why I am inclined to relate this to security, to the affirmation of his intact library, to its tangible physicality and accessibility, I'm not entirely sure.

FRAGMENTS, CONTINUED

'How is your work going?' my husband asks. 'Frustrating,' I reply. 'The thing I didn't realise about fragments is how completely you need to be able to articulate everything you choose not to include.' 'Ah yes,' he grins. 'You must know exactly what it is you are absolutely not saying.'

MARKING TIME

Decay and decline are commonly associated with Beckett's work. Along with failure, despair, negation, and absurdity. Back to that line by Anne Lamott: 'the redemption in Beckett is so small: in the second act of *Waiting for Godot*, the barren dying twig of a tree has put out a leaf. Just one leaf. It's not much; still Beckett didn't commit suicide. He wrote.'

And yet . . . And yet . . . 'Samuel Beckett has been read since the 1950s as a writer whose work is essentially anti-nihilist in nature,' critic Shane Weller tells us. Philosophers and critics point to the way that Beckett's characters engage in a performative struggle with nihilism in a way that can be read as a form of resistance to the inherent absurdity and meaninglessness of life.

Beckett denied that the leaf was a symbol of hope, of course. Just a way of marking time.

LE PETIT CHAGRIN

My husband almost entirely stops speaking in French, and so I try to keep up bilingualism on my own, in a language that is not mine. I invent a game to play in the car. Translate a line from a book or movie into French for others to guess where it originates. The children howl at my errors – I keep mixing up the order of adjectives and nouns, saying *stupide seau* ('bucket stupid') instead of *seau stupide* ('stupid bucket'). I translate 'battered hat' as *chapeau pourri*, 'rotten hat'. My son has his turn: 'Jusqu'a le petit chagrin a fini son diner,' he enunciates carefully. Everyone is quiet. 'Until the little sadness

77

finished his dinner?' my daughter translates. My son frowns. 'Oh,' he says. 'I thought *chagrin* meant kitten.'

COMPOSITION (PART III)

In *Dolly Parton, Songteller*, Parton tells the story of a night when she wrote two of her most famous hits:

> I had gained a lot of weight. I have a tendency to do that. At the time, I had tried everything to get the weight off, and there was this new diet out. It was like a liquid protein, and it was just the awfulest tasting stuff. You had to drink it three times a day, and you just gag when you are doing it. We were staying at a Howard Johnson's hotel. It had these great fried clams, which I loved. The band was down there in the restaurant. I could hear them laughing and talking. I was in my room, because I couldn't go down there and eat. I remember just feeling so sorry for myself in this lonely-ass room while they were having a party. I thought, 'Well, I can't eat. I can't just sit here and feel sorry for myself. Why don't I just write a song?'

I like Beckett's characters – I find their despair a comfort – but Dolly Parton resisting the horror of being on a terrible diet and feeling sorry for herself in a 'lonely-ass room' by writing two of the greatest songs of all time, well, that's something else entirely. That's more than resistance: that's closer to what I am inclined to think of as *being a fucking genius*.

ÉCOUTE

Some things in French are better than English. *Je t'écoute* is so much sharper and more satisfying than the drawn out *I am listening to you*, and I co-opt it sometimes when speaking to the children. *Oui, je t'écoute*, I enunciate as they take it in turns to tell me things, feeling the click of the consonants against my teeth.

Jean-Luc Nancy argues that listening is a philosophical stance. Whatever you say, say nothing, says Seamus Heaney.

Can you lose a language?

SOBRIETY (PART III)

In *Quit Like a Woman: The Radical Choice to Not Drink in a Culture Obsessed with Alcohol*, Holly Whitaker explains that Alcoholics Anonymous did not work for her as a pathway to sobriety because AA relies on a dissolution of the ego, a bowing down before a higher power: surrender. This is not, Whitaker suggests, a useful strategy for women whose egos are already decimated, women who are motivated to abuse alcohol because they crave some sort of *dissolving* of themselves. Whitaker proposes a different recovery program for modern women who want to quit booze: a program that relies on construction rather than deconstruction, on staking a claim for the self, on protection and reparation rather than dissolution. Rather than structuring your life around refusal, Whitaker suggests scaffolding. Instead of denial, build around yourself a life so rich that drinking becomes unnecessary.

COMPLIQUÉ

I trawl through French websites looking at silk camisoles and mohair jumpers and woollen coats, cotton dresses and chunky leather belts. I do it furtively, dishonestly, with guilt. It is a bourgeois habit, and a part of me despises myself when I start filling carts as if I am a wealthy executive rather than a struggling poet in lockdown, clicking on the *en soldes* and *petit prix* and *dernière chance*. I buy stupid things: a zebra-striped jumper, an expensive silk blouse, a t-shirt that has CIAO AMORE in buttercup-yellow Art Deco font. I fall in love with buttons and buckles and patterns. I send them to my sister-in-law in Rouen for her to post on to me, apologising, justifying. She understands: *C'est compliqué de résister aux pulls*, she texts in reply. 'It's hard to resist jumpers.'

'Without lubricating or looking away' – *n'importe quoi*.

ELSEWHERE (PART II)

I was never elsewhere, here is my only elsewhere.

> – Samuel Beckett, *The Unnamable*

VOICES (PART III)

When my children are at home their questions do not abate, and I must choose whether to answer them, or ask them to stop asking. The only thing I need to do with Beckett is pause the audio when I need a moment to recover from a line, like 'Did he love me then as much as I loved him? You never could be sure with that little hypocrite'. It is a comfort to be immersed in work written by a man who feels cursed to be a writer, who does not want to write, does not want to add his words to the shit heap of words that have already been written in the name of literature, but is driven relentlessly to create, working from memory, from instinct, despite himself.

Composition (Part IV)

I am looking after my son and his friend. My son's friend asks politely if I can show them a picture of the Himeji Castle in Japan. They want to draw it. The two six-year-old boys sit next to each other and begin to draw – the friend with a dark felt-tip pen, my son with a grey pastel. 'This is not good,' the friend says, critically. He glances at my son's picture and says with relief, 'Yours is not good either.' 'Mine is good,' says my son. The friend does not look convinced. 'We're not doing our best,' he explains. 'I'm doing my best,' my son replies. 'But it's not your *best* picture,' the friend says. 'Yes, it's the best. This is my best picture,' says my son. His friend does not finish his picture. My son asks me to photograph him standing with his wonky castle scratched onto the thick art paper, smiling proudly.

Questions (Part IV)

'Maman, is it déjà vu, or *danger* vu?'

Summer

It is increasingly clear I am not doing well. That despite the joyful company of Beckett's irascible, hilarious narrators, I am *doing poorly*.

Drowning in the endless chores, the pressures of parenting, the confusion of home-schooling, the anxiety about friends and family overseas, I am now shackled to a creative project that just won't let me be. I find myself writing on the edges of supermarket magazines, on the backs of receipts, on my children's drawings. I find myself always awake at 3am, bitterly practising yoga or scrawling in a notebook, weeping. I find myself desperate for something I cannot articulate. The things I write are increasingly nonsensical:

> The wide sky is blue, the day has been levered open like the lid off a tin of paint. But what, then, is the sky? The lid, the paint in the tin? Or the paint that clings to the lid when it is levered open for the first time with a screwdriver? Or does a new day have, in fact, nothing to do with a tin of paint? The day, after all, is not a sticky mess – not yet, perhaps not at all . . . ?

I write this sweating. (I write everything sweating). The hottest room in the house is the room no-one else will enter.

SOBRIETY (PART IV)

'One must be mad or drunk,' the Abbé Sieyès said, to speak well in the known languages. One must be drunk or mad, I should add, to dare, still, to use words, any word . . .

– Emil Cioran, *The Trouble with Being Born*

GOING ON

Beckett's obsession with *going and not going* is a constant refrain in his work. Over the summer I hear the thwarted goings and not goings of

Beckett's characters as exclamations of being physically rather than psychologically trapped: more like Nagg and Nell, legless in their rubbish bins, than Clov, threatening and struggling to leave his dying father. I, too, must go and cannot go, just like Jean Anderson in a TV adaptation of *Endgame*, her elegant face peeping out of the rubbish bin, reminiscing with a rapt expression about her time on Lake Como. The pandemic has us locked in a rubbish bin full of sand; we are trapped in a very straightforward way. We do not need existential or Freudian interpretations.

According to one critic, philosopher Theodor Adorno marked up his copy of *The Unnamable* with notes on Beckett's endless variations on the theme of 'going on':

> Adorno wrote elsewhere that 'through the seemingly Stoic "going on" is silently screamed that things should be different' . . . If you must go on and you cannot go on, and yet on you go, then you follow a path supremely difficult to chart, but not therefore meaningless.

I feel like this gets to the heart of it. We must go on and we cannot go on and yet on we go. What path, indeed, are we charting?

CONSTRUCTION

My daughter is building a cubby house outside in the damp autumn chill of early morning. If this were a school day, I'd have her inside eating breakfast, but schools have now been closed, and we're all in a state of lawlessness. Her cubby is unstable and keeps collapsing, the wet wood tumbling in on her. She is just outside the kitchen window and keeps howling with discontent. It grates on me, but I resist the urge to help or chastise her. She's young and cheerful – she won't keep returning to this collapsing house forever. She'll change strategy or walk away – find better wood, or an improved location. She has not been conditioned to believe that this shitty combination of bad material and inadequate design is all that she deserves.

AUDIBLE (PART II)

I find a small MP3 player at the bottom of a drawer. It has not been used for three years but I rustle up a charger and some headphones and clip it to my sports bra before I go for a run. It, too, like every other media player in our house, has been loaded up with the work of hundreds of French singer-songwriters. I remember when I could not discern much of the language. It was relaxing to be surrounded by oceans of melody that would pop with sudden comprehensible phrases – *je t'aime quand même* – *un bonbon qui colle* – *comme un poème!* – and then drift back into pleasant noise. Sometimes I changed the lyrics to ones I had initially misheard, and then preferred: I always replaced *j'ai tant besoin de toi* – 'I need you so much', with the infinitely more joyful, *j'ai pas besoin de toi* 'I do not need you.' Now I know too much, I understand too much; French is no longer pleasantly melodic, but jarringly comprehensible; another voice that denies silence, that demands attention. I return the music player to the drawer.

INTERRUPTIONS (PART IV)

My daughter comes to me with a mouthful of yoghurt. 'Maman, I have severe malofactories,' she says. 'I have a white tongue!' 'Go back to the table and finish your dinner!' I tell her. 'And *malofactory* is not a word.' 'Isn't it?' she snorts gleefully. My son hears and shouts from the table. 'Me too, I have malofactory!' My daughter laughs so much that yoghurt comes out of her nose.

I Google *malofactory*. It is not a word. There are lots of words that are close – malefactory, for example – but I don't think she thinks *malofactory* is actually a disease. I think she just had yoghurt on her tongue and a bunch of hilarious syllables in her mouth.

Silence (Part II)

Everyone looks in his own way for something that will cure the silence, the feeling of guilt, the feeling of panic. Some people travel. In their anxiety to see new countries and new people there is the hope that they will leave behind their own obscure ghosts; there is the secret hope that somewhere on earth they will find the one person who could talk to them.

– Natalia Ginzburg, 'Silence', *The Little Virtues*

Composition (Part V)

In 1920, Tristan Tzara explained how to compose a Dadaist poem: cut up the words from a newspaper article, place them in a bag and pull them out one by one, then copy them out in the order in which they left the bag. The result will be a poem that 'will resemble you', Tzara writes. 'And there you are – an infinitely original author of charming sensibility.'

Beckett produced a piece called *Lessness* in 1970, following a similar method – he wrote the sixty sentences himself, rather than cutting them out of a newspaper article, and he put them in a box rather than a bag, but then composed the piece by writing them in the order that he pulled them out of the box. He repeated the process, so that each sentence appears twice in the composition. Brater refers to this process as an example of Beckett 'slumming' rather than composing. I prefer to think of my found poem, the one gleaned from words my daughter underlined in a French parenting magazine, as resembling a version of me that is *infinitely original*, of *charming sensibility*.

Poem (Part II)

One night, waiting for my children to fall asleep, I sit on the edge of my son's bed looking at their toys in the corner of the dark bedroom. An enormous rubber blue diplodocus has been crammed into a doll's house, its huge meaty tail and long neck completely jack-knifed in order to fit. As I sit there in silence, looking at the poor oversized beast pressed up against the walls, hilariously unsuited to this tiny, domesticated space, I feel a sudden kinship.

'Maman: not a projection / made only of her class origins / containing an opus / must be solitary.'

Interruptions (Part V)

Because I make so many mistakes, my children begin to check everything I say. 'Just grab some bread,' I mutter one morning. 'Grain de blé? Maman? Did you say *grain de blé?*' 'No, I said, *grab some bread.*' 'Oh! That's funny! I thought you said grain de blé. Did you hear me, Maman? Did you hear that? I thought you said, grain de blé!' 'Grain de blé?' my other child asks, coming into the kitchen. 'Why are you talking about grain de blé?'

Grain de blé simply means 'grain of wheat', and there is really no conceivable reason I would be using this term in the kitchen, mid-morning, with my children. But they don't have preconceived notions of what I am likely to be saying to them at any point in time. This is both exasperating and liberating – they are listening, attentive, ready. Because they do not expect me to say one thing over another, the ear hears what the ear hears, and how am I to argue with that? I know it is my responsibility to enunciate – I need to be more intentional with my words, to stop making so many mistakes, stop mumbling. But I feel as if I am constantly speaking, constantly required to make sense, to articulate, to explicate, and it all just takes so much *fucking energy*.

> I fear we are not getting rid of God because we still believe in grammar.
>
> – Friedrich Nietzsche, *Twilight of the Idols*

ELSEWHERE (PART III)

Beckett, in 1954, was asked about the authors who had shaped him. He discounted Kafka, and then wrote that he did not mean to imply that he was 'resistant to influences', continuing, 'I merely note that I have always been a poor reader, incurably inattentive, on the look-out for an elsewhere. And I think I can say, in no spirit of paradox, that the reading experiences which have affected me most are those that were best at sending me to that elsewhere.'

VOICES (PART IV)

'What are you doing?' my son asks. 'I am just looking up a word,' I mutter. 'What word is it?' he asks. 'Intercalated,' I reply, scrolling quickly through the definition. My daughter bursts into the room, her clothes ripped for a zombie costume. She is holding a ukulele and a stick. 'I will play you a song!' she shouts, positioning the stick as a bow on her makeshift violin. She saws back and forth as my son howls with laughter.

I could have said the word was *dialogic*, or *polyphonic*. The effect would have been the same. But it would not have been the truth.

GOING ON (PART II)

Estragon: Let's go.
Vladimir: We can't.
Estragon: Why not?
Vladimir: We're waiting for Godot.

– Samuel Beckett, *Waiting for Godot*

INTERRUPTIONS (PART VI)

Maman, is infinity a number?

FUCK OFF

There's a scene in Beckett's *Malone Dies* that haunts me – a scene that also occurs, in various guises, in *Company*, and also in an earlier short story called 'The End'. (Recurrence as haunting). In *Malone Dies*:

I said, The sky is further away than you think, is it not, mama? It was without malice, I was simply thinking of all the leagues that separated me from it. She replied, to me her son, It is precisely as far away as it appears to be. She was right. But at the time I was aghast.

In *Company*:

Looking up at the blue sky and then at your mother's face you break the silence asking her if it is not in reality much more distant than it appears. The sky that is. The blue sky. Receiving no answer you mentally reframe your question and some hundred paces later look up at her face again and ask her if it does not appear much less distant than in reality it is. For some reason you could never fathom this question must have angered her exceedingly. For she shook off your little hand and made you a cutting retort you have never forgotten.

In 'The End':

A small boy, stretching out his hands and looking up at the blue sky, asked his mother how such a thing was possible. Fuck off, she said.

I present these texts not in the order that Beckett wrote them (first 'The End', followed by *Malone Dies*, and then *Company*) but in the order I came across them. In my discovery of them the violence of the mother increases – the little boy is wounded in the first fragment, but his mother's response is not cruel, just a little snappy. The depiction of a sensitive little boy 'aghast' at her response is comic, even. In *Company* she shakes off his hand, physically irritated, and makes a cutting retort that, in 'The End', becomes the improbable and hilarious 'Fuck off'.

I am haunted by this scene because I position myself, of course, as the mother, and the mother of a sensitive, curious little boy who is sometimes on the pointy end of my fatigue or irritation. In these scenes, I experience the little boy as a violence against his mother – weary and emotional, withstanding the sustained attack of endless, unanswerable questions. 'Is not the sky in reality much more distant than it appears?' is the kind of question that might highlight, uncomfortably, one's own inadequate knowledge, but is also, in its sheer grammatical complexity, a question that requires a degree of energy and ingenuity one cannot always access. When my son asks me, seriously, 'What is the opposite of Wednesday?' I sometimes want to kneel on the ground and weep with frustration.

Nostalgia (Part V)

Regretting – that's what helps you on . . . regretting what is, regretting what was . . . that's what transports you, towards the end of regretting.

– Samuel Beckett, *The Unnamable*

More Aphorisms

'It's surprisingly hard to write an aphorism,' my nihilism professor once said. Sometimes I still think about him sitting down and licking the tip of a pencil, ready to write 'an aphorism'. I think of it a little bit like a gag cartoon – one panel, him at a handsome mahogany desk, tongue between his teeth, the page full of scribbled-out attempts to get the correct wording:

~~It's hard to write~~
~~It's so hard to write~~
~~It is not easy~~
~~Aphorisms are surprisingly~~
       surprisingly
   It's   ^   *hard to write an aphorism*

Voices (Part V)

Daughter: I wish I could hear the Mona Lisa sing.
Son: Yes. I wonder what her voice sounds like.

Kinderlaufbergeist?

During a camping trip we take a hike up a mountain in the ranges of the north and on the way back down our children run, screaming Beethoven's fifth. 'Beethoven is rolling in his grave!' my husband sighs. 'Do you think,' I ask, 'there is a German word that means "the music of children as they run screaming down a mountain after a long hike"?'

Tenter de vivre

We watch a Japanese animation called *The Wind Rises* and that night, the wind rises, shuddering in the blinds and shaking the doors. I cannot sleep. *Le vent se lève; il faut tenter de vivre* is the refrain of the film, a line from the work of poet Paul Valéry – 'the wind rises; we must try to live'.

*

91

I cannot quite describe the solace I find in Beckett; the meditative quality of listening to his work as I drown in chores and responsibilities. I think the solace is visceral, somatic. The relief of returning to inhabit your body after a long, exhausting illness that has had you locked up and jittery in the corridors of your brain. I think when I listen to Beckett I am listening to something that rumbles like a distant train, pressing my ear to the track.

> . . . perhaps that's what I feel, myself vibrating, I'm the tympanum, on the one hand the mind, on the other hand the world, I don't belong to either . . .
>
> — Samuel Beckett, *The Unnamable*

What muscular pleasure am I accessing in plugging myself into the voice of an earnest madman, one bent upon articulating his own impotence? Is this the path we are charting – inward?

The wind is rattling the doors, making them unpick themselves from their frames and slowly rattle in the suck and puff of the house. I use words like suck and puff because I have been reading Beckett; I no longer use *inhale* and *exhale* like a fool who does not understand the physicality of the wind. There is madness, still, in all of this. In the unpicking. In the waiting. I do not expect it to be of any concern to anyone. We shall see.

Going On (Part III)

'I couldn't have done it otherwise. Gone on, I mean. I could not have gone through the awful wretched mess of life without having left a stain upon the silence.'

— Samuel Beckett, cited by biographer Deirdre Bair

Interruptions (Part VII)

'Maman, do you know about the Pig Dream? I dreamed that it rained and rained until our back garden became a pond, full of tadpoles and salamanders. And on our front porch was a tiny little pig.'

'Oh!' I reply in delight. 'A tiny little pig,' I repeat, smiling.

Voices (Part VI)

Once, my husband was working on preparing a parade to launch a big arts festival. 'Some children came to visit the floats today,' he told me. 'They were blind, and they came backstage to feel the floats before the parade, so they could get a sense of what they looked like. They ran their hands all over the floats and chatted excitedly to each other about what they could feel.'

True

'I don't have a sense of what you and your husband do for a living,' an editor once commented on my work. 'Just the usual artistic precarity,' I wanted to reply. 'We do what we love, we teach what we love, and we have a million other random jobs to pay the rent.' Guillaume's vocational trajectory is particularly hard to map because he is crippled by restlessness, like me. His life story contains more than I have ever, myself, been able to grasp. I only found out he could speak Spanish after five years together when I came across him speaking Spanish with a couple he'd just met at a party. Another time, he came home and told me he was going to play drums for a new band and when I said, 'You can't play the drums,' he just shrugged and replied, 'Yeah, I can.'

A lot of things about what Guillaume 'does for a living' are true. If I told you he's an academic, that would be true. That he has a penchant for blazers, wears a lanyard, likes to work with volunteers – those things would also be true. That he has a forklift, truck and motorbike licence. That he studied jazz in Paris. Plays bass. Composed the soundtrack to a successful Vietnamese film. Wrote his PhD thesis on Japanese zombies. Has been a nude artist's model, a ski instructor, a cattle musterer, a kitchen chef, the guy who collects the trolleys at the supermarket, the guy digging holes with a pressure hose for the new carpark at the airport. It would all be true, true, true. Now he works in community radio and teaches film studies and never seems to mind that nobody knows how eccentric he is, how unmappable his life has been. His not minding is, to me, one of the strangest things about him. As if part of me believes he did it all for it all to be known, rather than just doing it to do it.

SILENCE (PART III)

Auden tells us that in the poet's study, silence is turned into objects. Beckett has Molloy say, on the other hand, that 'to restore silence is the role of objects'. I know, each time I consider buying something, French clothes, the Japanese dress, that I am attempting to buy silence – I am trying to quiet the noise of suspension, of expectation, of waiting, that is screaming for release.

'I use the words you taught me,' Clov says to Hamm. 'If they don't mean anything anymore, teach me others! Or let me be silent.'

After a while I start to answer the enervating, eccentric questions. 'What's inside a lizard?' my son asks. 'An umbrella,' I tell him. He looks back at me with respect, for my engagement in *n'importe quoi*.

ADDENDA

One of Beckett's addenda at the end of *Watt* reads:

> for all the good that frequent departures out of Ireland had done him, he might just as well have stayed there.

I underline it twice. I am using a small Japanese postcard as a bookmark. The postcard is a nineteenth-century print by Hiroshige Andō called 'The Plum Garden in Kameido'. It shows delicate plum blossoms on gnarled, hardy grey trees, with tiny figures visiting in the background. The plum trees are fenced, so that people know where they are allowed to walk when visiting the garden. Visiting the blossoms is a seasonal activity in Japan and is known as *hanami*. Cherry blossoms, or *sakura*, have cultural significance – they represent the transience of life, fleeting joy and beauty. At the end of a dark winter the trees blossom, for a moment, and then are scattered by spring winds and rain, and the trees revert back to their ordinary state: trunks, boughs, leaves.

TRUE (PART II)

'I was never a ski instructor,' Guillaume reminds me. 'I was a breakfast cook at a ski resort, and a sales assistant at a rental ski shop. But not a ski instructor. That's not true.'

GOING AND NOT GOING

Vladimir: Well? Shall we go?
Estragon: Yes, let's go.

They do not move.
Curtain.

THE END

– Samuel Beckett, *Waiting for Godot*

Twenty Segments
of Waiting

All waiting is a joke in which you are the punchline. If you refuse to ridicule your own plight, if you decide to reject the absurdity of suspension, you must replace it with something else. Madness, fury, delusion. Godot does not arrive, of course. But he *might*.

*

Here is the simplest form of waiting: waiting for something you are certain will arrive, something with a predetermined arrival date. A package you have sent yourself: some linen sleepwear, perhaps, in dove grey. (Fun fact: a person who has ordered linen sleepwear in dove grey is not going to wait serenely. This person is attempting to *purchase* serenity). The degree of impatience attached to the waiting will be determined by the extent to which you believe that you, personally, will be improved by the delivery. Will this sleepwear improve your outlook, your mood, your mettle?

*

You can also wait for objects that may or may not arrive – unpurchased objects, say, like an inexplicably heavy gift from your mother or a missive from an unrequited love. This may depend on how often you receive gifts, or letters – the extent of the expectation that you have attached to waiting for the unexpected. Perhaps an empty mailbox is an insult to you. Maybe you check it compulsively, scowling at the empty chamber three times a day as if it is mocking your lack, delighting in your unresolved ache, Derrida muttering *attendre sans s'attendre*, 'wait without expecting', in your ear. Again, in this example, it is only the object that will ever arrive, or not arrive.

*

You can wait for a reply to a declaration. You can wait for a return on any kind of vulnerability, any kind of exposure you may have made. This can be the most excruciating and the most exquisite type of waiting: if you are feeling stagnant, this will make you feel unbearably alive. You will marvel at your self-control in not pitching yourself headfirst down a flight of stairs. You will contemplate online gambling – anything in which the return is immediate, the destruction palpable. Like gambling, though, this kind of waiting can become addictive – the rush of return, the despair of silence.

*

You can wait for someone, either at a predetermined place you have agreed to meet, or without their knowledge, because you have memorised their schedule and know that on Tuesdays they have a break between classes and usually head across the bridge to the main campus for lunch. In the case of the latter, you must hide your waiting. You can do this by stopping to look for something in your bag or strolling slowly whilst gazing in the opposite direction to which you expect them – preferably at the mountains in the distance, low and misty in the last days of autumn. It is easy to pretend that you have not been waiting: what is hard is to engage the one you have waited for in an interaction meaningful enough to alleviate the shame of the concealed waiting.

*

Your waiting may also depend on how you were treated as a child, whether or not your mother and aunt spent afternoons trying to get your attention so that they could win a point in the game 'Who Is the Baby Looking At?' when the music stopped. This sort of thing, as an example, might skewer your expectations as an adult – enthusiastically vying for a baby's regard could result in that baby believing, as a grown woman, that she is the deserving and enduring focus of all adult attention. Any deviation from this blueprint might be unsettling; could lead to irritable waiting for a return to the native state in which she is the centre of all conscious attention.

*

You can wait for bad things to pass; you can wait for bad things to happen. These types of waiting seem different, and we give them different names – one of these is forbearance, the other anxiety. But they share a skin, they slip between states.

*

You can forget that you are waiting until you open your phone to find a text from an unknown number that begins, *It is almost impossible to admit but* . . . and cities collapse within you as, shaking, you open the text only to find it is an invitation to a birthday party that continues, *. . . I am about to turn fifty and want you to join me to celebrate!* The note is certainly not a declaration of reciprocated yearning from a confusing past hurt, a ghost you have tried to forget, a married colleague from many years ago that you were not supposed to fall in love with, whose schedule you were never meant to memorise . . . In a case like this, the waiting has been going on behind the scenes, has learned to be silent. This kind of waiting can congeal with time, can form a plateau that seems solid enough to build upon. You can construct a world on top of all that silenced anticipation, and you won't even know until one day a text creates an earthquake and swallows it all up in a heartbeat. And then you will see the ravenous

99

maw of wait and know that you have to starve it back underground again.

*

Waiting is a mood, a delusion, an insult, a harbinger, a tangle, an embarrassment. It is a cocktail of entitlement and fear, a suspended relapse. It is a yearning for violence, it is both concave and repellent. It is an impatience, a gnawing inability, the lurking threat of both becoming and unbecoming.

*

Waiting is breathtaking, transformative arrest.

*

You can wait for confirmation. For mysteries to be solved. For the track to be selected, for the random order of things to make sense. You can wait for patterns to be revealed, for the other shoe to drop. You can wait for wars to end, for plagues to end, for embargoes to be lifted, for sentences to be served, for presidencies to terminate, for cases to be dismissed. You can wait for a narrative arc to emerge, for direction, for any kind of foothold.

*

Waiting can ruin your life, if your life needs ruining.

*

Waiting is a form of impatience with the status quo – it is a restlessness for something that has an unknown tense – a sort of conditional *perhaps / not yet*. All waiting is internal – it comes from a perceived lack, a deficit. But you can also wait for things that can only happen inside of you: to heal after grief, or to get over someone, for example. You can wait to be an instigator, to clarify your curiosity, to make the first move, to get things right. To be honest and upfront about your feelings. This may seem more like prevarication than waiting,

100

but it's not. Sometimes you have to be a different person to get things right, and that sort of waiting can last a lifetime.

*

You cannot speed up waiting. You cannot terminate waiting. Waiting is an unwanted state in which you have zero control. There is nothing to be learned in waiting, except dogged perseverance of the waiting, and a kind of gentle awareness that you should not think too much about that game that your mother and your aunt played when you were a baby, and how that may now have ruined all your attempts at love. Waiting is not the time to interrogate yourself about why you couldn't admit that you were waiting for him, the married colleague you fell so inexplicably and inextricably in love with, or why you lived for years longing to know how he felt yet refusing to ask, refusing to hint. Because an affair would have been just a different type of waiting, and nobody should ever fall in love with waiting.

*

Waiting can be very passive, to the point of apathy. You can wait for financial stability, as if one day you will wake up as someone who values financial stability. You can wait for your body to change, holding on to the jeans you bought fifteen years ago, as if you can change the disposition of your body and the allocation of mass. You can go even further than this and wait for things that will never happen, wait for Gong Yoo to ask you to ghostwrite his autobiography. Only the very arrogant, however, would label this a form of waiting.

*

You can wait to give birth. That is every type of waiting rolled into one.

*

You can wait to be a better kind of person, a better wife or mother or daughter. This is particularly internal and particularly passive, because motherhood, especially, does not come easily to everyone, and the waiting can feel senseless, unachievable. In the case of motherhood, endurance can be a more useful framework than waiting. Sometimes you simply need to make a thousand vegemite sandwiches and bathe the children fourteen hundred times and help them hold their pencils before the cog finally engages and shifts that behemoth mechanical structure to emit the required torque to make a mother.

*

I need not say that this sort of waiting is more profound than waiting for a package of linen pyjamas in dove grey. By the time the pyjamas arrive you have already forgotten that there was ever a lack, was ever something you yearned for, was ever a way in which you felt inadequate. Sometimes it's nice just to order something and know that it will arrive. Some things you wait for don't.

*

The relationship between reality and delusion can be difficult to ascertain while waiting. That's part of the discomfort. How can you get a grip on how realistic your expectations are without calling into question your own sanity? Waiting can be split open, like a mandarin, but how can you tell which segment you are holding? Waiting as comedy. Waiting as anticipation, as expectation. Waiting as exposure, or longing. Waiting as pathological. Waiting as the result of fear. Waiting as an illusion, as a mood. Waiting versus 'change as constant'. Waiting versus 'closure as myth'. Waiting as both nihilism and opportunity. Waiting as perfect failure. Waiting as acceptance – or, waiting as entitlement. Waiting as procreation. Waiting as inevitable. Waiting as clumsy transference. Waiting as delusion – waiting as life-force. Waiting can be a trial, both for and against your ability to identify what is reasonable and what is, effectively, madness.

*

It is not impossible that waiting unhinges you precisely because your hinges were so loose to begin with. Your mother dug a trench to shock you out of her overdue womb, a ten-foot trench with a pick-axe in the wide heat of Queensland's tropical summer. She smashed through the earth, her belly swinging in an arc, until you came along. Which you did. Came into a world of abundance and wonder, in which you lacked for nothing: not for love, not for food, not for company, not for a wild mother who would teach you how to hold on to your rage, your own furious fate. You were born to wrangle with waiting, to resist the cage of quietism. No small wonder then, that you hate to wait.

Moon Overhead,
Nothing Moving

Fourteen months after I first started keeping a research folder labelled 'NIHILISM' I found myself standing in the kitchen of our two-bedroom apartment clutching a letter from the local council that said our demolition plans had been approved.

I'd been keeping the research folder in a listless attempt to claw my way back to a point in my life that had seemed full of radical potential, a time before living in the suburbs and parenting small children and teaching online. The research was an effort to reacquaint myself with the sense of violent eradication and renunciation that had accompanied the wild freedom of my university days in Paris, days in which a *revaluation of all values* had seemed not only possible but imminent.

I am, naturally, an eradicator. I like to tear holes in the fabric of my life and climb through them. I have moved continents eight times as part of an ongoing hustle (*compulsion?*) to set fire to my life, obliterate it all, strip, raze, incinerate any sense of familiarity in order to re-establish myself, my expectations, my perspectives, leaving behind lovers, friends, jobs, furniture, plants and books. It is not hard. You hug tight. You shuck it off.

This is a common enough instinct in ex-pat circles, it does not seem weird amongst international students or ESL teachers who live abroad or those who are born restless and perpetually relocating far from their origins, people who feel that their only belonging is 'elsewhere', people who understand the German term *Fernweh* – the opposite of homesickness, the state of longing for somewhere else.

I have spent most of my adult life in these communities, giving away furniture and cleaning supplies and accepting them gratefully, upon arrival in a new city, from those who were moving on. It is only when I come back to my hometown of Adelaide that all of this movement seems bizarre, reckless, even pathological.

Eight times is a little excessive, *quand même.*

This is the thing, though – the true thing – about that letter. It was my house, but they were not my demolition plans.

I stood with the letter in my hand, thinking, *Our lease expires in January – we are in the middle of a pandemic – it's nearly Christmas – my husband has not finished his thesis – the children go to school just around the corner – there's a housing crisis – our house is going to be demolished – I can look up the plans online – I can look up the plans online – they're going to build two three-bedroom townhouses on our block, each with a garage and a lap pool.* I kept repeating this out loud – 'a lap pool!' – as if it captured my anguish.

'Our home is going to be bulldozed,' I began to tell people. I was intently focused on the bulldozing because the scheduled destruction of my home felt acutely visceral. I wanted to tell people that we were being forced to move, but more than that, that I anticipated the demolition on a somatic level, as if the house was an extension of my physical self, of my children's selves. I wanted to tell them that I could feel the arum lilies being torn up, the sprawling jade plant being demolished. That I could feel the churning of the clay-red soil, the splitting of the enormous jasmine vine, the way its roots would rip up the lizard sanctuary that my son and I had built one afternoon when he was home sick from school. I could feel the tiles on the roof come crashing down in slippery batches. The tearing of the old, threadbare carpet, the crumbling of the walls, the obliteration of the doorframes etched with the little notches that marked my children's heights.

As the weeks passed the garden ran wild and I developed a sickening awareness of the privilege of all my ruptures, all my fleeing. I did not want to move; I felt resistant and mulish. I realised with unpleasant clarity that I was not really into Nietzschean nihilism, revaluation, and destruction of the status quo if someone else was doing the destroying, if someone else was holding the flamethrower. Nietzsche advocates nihilism as a way of clearing out space, creating a vacuum, establishing a blank slate from which the poet-philosopher of the future can begin to conceive of and articulate new values, either for herself or for society at large. 'Nihilism is . . . not only the belief that everything deserves to perish; but one actually puts one's shoulder to the plough,' he explains. 'One destroys.'

I told myself that I'd begun to look into Nietzsche's writings for what might be found in the new dawn now that 'the old god is dead', for how an active nihilist might harness art, and poetry, as a way of establishing meaning and purpose in a meaningless world, but really I think I was looking for validation of my own compulsive fleeing, trying to unpick the knot to figure out what was a genetic predisposition for one-way tickets, what was philosophical investigation and what was just a perverse desire for implosion. I was also trying to interrogate my desire to make something of aesthetic value, trying to decide what I wanted to make now that I was forced to sit still rather than just jump on another plane.

I had the vague sense that I might like to try to build from the rubble, rather than just draw up blueprints, for the first time in my life, and in the middle of this strange and weird project *my fucking house was going to be demolished.* All this effort to learn how to live a life without fleeing, detonating, razing it all and starting again, only to come home to a letter telling me that this same thing would be done to me, that I would be forced to gut my life, strip my home, re-establish myself and my family again in new surroundings.

Does it matter how the conditions of nihilism are established – whether you *put your shoulder to the plough*, as Nietzsche puts it? Is the only thing that matters what you do *after the rupture* – the courage and commitment that you bring to the revaluation of all values?

It feels pretty disgusting to have your life annihilated. I want to say that Nietzsche does not belong to the world of those made homeless, those whose worlds are razed for them, but he is a passionate advocate of the necessity of pain and suffering:

> To those human beings who are of any concern to me I wish suffering, desolation, sickness, ill-treatment, indignities – I wish that they should not remain unfamiliar with profound self-contempt, the torture of self-mistrust, the wretchedness of the vanquished: I have no pity for them, because I wish them the only thing that can prove today whether one is worth anything or not – that one endures.

The wretchedness of the vanquished. As a man who suffered terribly throughout his life, it's not surprising to find that suffering is also the gravitational force of Nietzsche's writings on art, poetry, and creation – for Nietzsche, creating eases the pain of life, but a creator cannot create unless forged by the fires of misery, heartache, and agony:

> Creation – that is the great redemption from suffering, and life's easement. But that the creator may exist, that itself requires suffering and much transformation. Yes, there must be much bitter dying in your life, you creators! Thus you are advocates and justifiers of all transitoriness . . . Truly, I have gone my way through a hundred souls and through a hundred cradles and birth-pangs.

I have taken many departures, I know the heart-breaking last hours. But my creative will, my destiny, wants it so. Or, to speak more honestly: my will wants precisely such a destiny.

This is all to explain how I ended up in an apron perched on a cardboard box full of books with my laptop balanced on my knees, intently tapping out a brief email to a friend I had not seen since we were both students in Paris over a decade ago. I cannot explain why contacting Alexandra suddenly seemed so urgent that I peeled off my dishwashing gloves in the middle of scrubbing the laundry floor and hunted through packed bags for my laptop charger and balanced on the edge of a box full of books to write to her. It is not as though I was lonely (I often think of myself as the opposite of lonely – regularly denied my quota of solitude). It is not as though we were close (I had not heard from her for over five years). It is not as though I had nothing else to do. Maybe it was the boxes. Maybe it was the demolition, the gutting. Maybe it was being fed up with Nietzsche, feeling old and mulish and hardened in my ways, the shame of my sudden confrontation with passive, rather than active, nihilism.

I sent my words out into the ether like ectoplasm, to track her down, to haunt her. I sent the message in the middle of the day, not knowing if it would find her in her morning, her evening, or the middle of her night, but hoping to hook her somewhere. In the email I promised her nothing except to *hit send*.

There is an expectation that time will improve you, consolidate you, but perhaps I wrote to Alex because I did not like the parts of myself that had hardened – I preferred the rubbery, slippery, liminal parts – the parts of me that were most alive in Paris. Alex and I were never refined together; we were rough sketches, first drafts of ourselves. We had met at the prestigious French university where I was studying terror and nihilism and she was actively immersed in feminist theory and questions of sexuality and gender. We were both freakishly studious. Alex stayed up all night researching intersectional feminism and I read dozens of books about Dionysus and scrawled poems in the margins of my notebooks.

Alexandra's final thesis on femininity featured a photograph of our bare legs stretched out towards the Seine near Pont Neuf, the lights of the Left Bank shimmering in the water. I don't remember when the photograph was taken; it could have been any of the countless afternoons of stretching and chatting, of vague attempts at inebriation, of sunshine and loitering and lazy refusal to experience anything Paris might have offered us except a spot near the Seine, our own rolled cigarettes, a forgotten bookstore, a bar for old men. We became experts in the sort of lounging inertia that takes over when you spend your time alone thinking and writing, and time together becomes a hallowed space of honeyed exhaustion. We tried to be so smart apart that it was a relief to be indolent together. Those moments are worth more now than any of the essays we wrote, the photograph of our legs stretched out on the banks of the Seine of greater value to both of us than either of our dissertations.

L'enfer c'est le déménagement, Alexandra replies swiftly – '*hell is moving house*' – from amidst her own upheaval. She is also gutting and folding and stacking and smoothing down the tops of boxes. We cobble together a correspondence as if we are both throwing bricks into the centre of a paddock, from opposite sides, hoping to build a wall. We do not say, 'I am so sorry' or 'I am so busy'. These phrases mean nothing to those who are relentlessly sorry, relentlessly busy. We commit to *the sending of the thing* without edit, without perfecting.

And so it is like this that I get fragments of her life that do not make exact chronological sense, that are scraggly and rangy and scattered and spontaneous. The first comes as she is moving house in New York, across a bridge, in pieces. Stupidly. As I am moving houses, in pieces, stupidly, from one street in my hometown to a street half a kilometre south. Of course we are both moving stupidly; this is the first time either of us have moved without getting on a plane. I tell her that I think I have moved half an onion that was in the door of the fridge.

The next email I receive from her is from her apartment in Greece. The logistics of her transition from New York to Athens are not clear – just part of the restlessness of her intercontinental life. She tells me that her days are dark and disorderly, makes a comment about how bleak she sounds, and then continues:

> *i blame the heat. i'm sitting on my balcony in athens, moon overhead, nothing moving. i think i've worked out that the stiller my surroundings, the more frantic my thoughts. i've had a lot of those days recently.*
>
> *i am also chainsmoking, which i thought i'd left in the past, because . . . because. because no one smokes anymore, because it's terrible for you, because until recently i was a serious runner.*

Over the next few days, I think of Alex, on the balcony in muggy Athens, chain-smoking, watching the moon overhead, nothing moving. I think about moving, about not moving, about nothing moving. It keeps coming back to me as I flatten down packing tape on cardboard boxes and wipe dust from windowsills. I think of her as I hose down the pavement and pull up the thyme in the garden to replant it in a large terracotta pot, as I snap off fragments of the jade plant and repot the spider plants and the bougainvillea, as I save my plants one by one from destruction.

The winter feels especially bitter, and I feel colder than I have ever been, colder than any of the winters I spent in Europe or East Asia. I try to worry about Alex's chain-smoking. I find nothing. *There is a part of me that is always chain-smoking on a balcony in muggy Athens,* I write back. *This part of me affirms all of your choices.*

Nietzschean nihilism is easy to instrumentalise but also maddeningly slippery. Destroy! Be courageous! Do not submit! Embrace pain! Create! I'm not sure I've got a handle on it yet – I'm not sure I ever will. I wonder if that is part of the appeal. I go back to *Thus Spoke Zarathustra*. I rise at dawn to read because there is no other time in the day. But perhaps also because I like to see the moon overhead, nothing moving. Zarathustra does not trust the moon, calling it a 'timid night-reveller' and a 'tomcat on the roofs', accusing it of slinking around and peering deceitfully at people, 'lustful for the earth and for all the joys of lovers'. He uses this image of the dishonest, silent moon to condemn those who refuse to acknowledge their earthly desires, those who claim to believe in 'pure knowledge'. He scorns their quiet contemplation as 'emasculated leering'. He contrasts these philosophers with their 'intoxicated moon-eyes' against his beloved, courageous, sublime, loving sun. One of the interesting elements of Nietzschean poetics is the way that his work resists paraphrase – what he says is only half as glorious as the way he says it:

> Piously and silently he walks along on star-carpets: but I do not like soft-stepping feet on which not even a spur jingles. Every honest man's step speaks out: but the cat steals along over the ground. Behold, the moon comes along catlike and without honesty.

Alexandra on a balcony in muggy Athens, chain-smoking. The moon hanging still in the oppressive heat of August. There is something hedonistic and life-affirming in this image that calls to me. I feel like her yin, her inverse, her southern shadow. I am brittle and icy, painstakingly sober. I feel like my entrails are frozen. But we are both awake before dawn, refusing to be balanced. I cling to this as I move house, watching the same moon as I consider what it means to be forced into a new existence.

First Light

Poets lie

Everything I tell you from this point on will be a lie.

Moon as companion

Our new house has three bedrooms, and I do not give the third to my daughter, who desperately wants a room of her own. Instead, it becomes my study. My desk looks out over the garden and each morning I rise before dawn to work. When I pull back the curtains, I see my face reflected in the window. The night pools against the lit room and I see myself, the room I am sitting in, tangled amongst the bare branches of fruit trees, one fierce star caught in a storage box above my head.

The moon is always there, blinking at me. The room faces west, and the sun rises from the mountains behind me to the east. I witness deep night lighten into day, a few pink clouds, a disappearing star. The fruit trees have not been pruned, and the branches are ragged at the top, unruly, many-fingered. I feel that I am watching the night fade, rather than the day arrive.

The sun's zenith

It is late winter. Each bleary-eyed morning, as I sit at my desk with a pot of green tea and a sliced apple, I take a photograph of the dawn and I read Nietzsche. I keep two sets of notes – notes on art, artistry, and creating, and another random collection of bits I like. Bits about islands and fig trees, about casting his nets into the sea only to draw up the heads of old gods, about freedom, and fishing. I keep note of Nietzsche's sun in particular – the heady warmth of Zarathustra's sun, the prophets who are fools for not laying down in it, for not luxuriating in the golden light. Nietzsche deploys this sun throughout his work as a metaphor for enlightenment, for possibility, for opportunity, its zenith as his 'great noon-tide' of new values and new meaning. The light of the sun exposes and clarifies in ways that are both exhilarating and terrifying.

My toes are always cold. My body cannot remember summer, heatwaves, bushfires, mosquitoes, or sunburn.

Fruit trees

No one can identify the fruit trees in the backyard. 'You'll have to see them through a season,' says the tree guy. He shows my husband his tattoo – a huge French flag, inked proudly on his inner forearm. 'I love the French,' he explains. 'He kept saying that,' my husband shrugs later. '*The French.*' The tree guy's tattoo mystifies me but belongs to the realm of impossible human mysteries. The trees on the other hand – the trees are an earthly mystery, a garden mystery, promising an explicating eruption of blossom. I check them daily – the closest to me has small white buds emerging – the other two remain bare, silent.

First light

Each morning is beautiful in a different way.

Some mornings the moon is so bright it looks like a hole in the fabric of the sky, white light streaming through the rupture. When it is bright like this it looks particularly planetary, particularly celestial. The moon will not leave the sky as the day arrives, does not believe in day, or night. Will not conform to its role as night-time light, guardian of darkness. Sometimes it seems swollen and close to the earth, other times an impossibly distant companion.

Nietzsche's poet-prophet Zarathustra often speaks to the dawn as he grapples with his destiny, either waking with the dawn or addressing it after a sleepless night. The 'blushing sky' brings with it an obligation, a reckoning. The night, inarticulate and monstrous, has challenged Zarathustra to leave his haven – his solitary mountain cave or his companions on the 'blissful isles' – and continue his difficult journey to speak and to act, to uncover and disseminate his prophecies. There is a sense of terror in these moments, of fierce honesty and desperate reflection.

The sun is rising, *we must try to live.*

Who has not been awake, in turmoil, to speak to the dawn?

As I continue to rise early a line by the Canadian poet Christian Bök returns to me again and again. *Minds grim with nihilism still find first light inspiring.* Bök's line comes from his work *Eunoia*, an ambitious and impressive Oulipian poetic endeavour in which he commits to only using one vowel per chapter. 'Nihilism' is a good word for the Chapter 'I' – multiple syllables, only the sanctioned vowel. I find it disorienting that this line, the one that haunts me, was composed as part of a playful and daring exercise in poetics. I feel as if it contains something essential, some kernel of wisdom, a truth that is trying to will itself into existence.

Nihilism, and the affirmation of life

Nietzsche, besides his blissful isles and fig trees and luxuriating sun, is a philosopher whose work is steeped in nihilism, although there are disagreements about the extent to which Nietzsche is a philosopher of nihilism or anti-nihilism or a diagnostician of nihilism or a prophet, oracle, poet, advocate, enemy of nihilism. That his mind was *grim with nihilism* is even matter for debate – grim? Or gleeful?

Nietzsche is, I would argue, the most fun of the nihilists: hilarious, petty, unsystematic, and intentionally offensive with his use of the term. He swings it like a mace and chain at his big enemies – those he sees as being 'anti-life': Christian moralists and some of the major philosophers, particularly Schopenhauer – but also, when he pleases, at anyone who shits him. He calls Flaubert a nihilist, for example, because Flaubert wrote that one can only think and write properly when sitting, exclaiming:

> Now I have you, nihilist! Assiduity is the *sin* against the holy spirit. Only ideas *won by walking* have any value.

Nietzsche responds to his gallery of nihilists with that which he believes *affirms* life in the face of these moral systems, philosophers and writers who insist on negating it with their damaging claims to truth, knowledge, and sitting.

The affirmation of life that art provides is a clear theme of Nietzsche's from his earliest published works and private note-books through to the last. We can see this positioning of art as a counterforce to nihilism when Nietzsche argues that the genuine Christian – i.e., the most dangerous nihilist – harbours anti-artistic sentiments; when he identifies poetry and creating as that which can redeem us from our suffering; when he calls art the 'highest task', and that which makes life both possible and worth living; when he refers to himself, as a poet and a philosopher, as both a 'pessimist and art-deifier'.

In his 'Attempt at a Self-Criticism', the foreword that accompanied later publications of his first book, *The Birth of Tragedy*, Nietzsche offers art-making as the only truly metaphysical activity of man, that which goes beyond morality, beyond good and evil. Nietzsche questions if morality might be 'a will to negate life . . . a secret instinct of annihilation, a principle of decay, diminution and slander – the beginning of the end? Hence, the danger of dangers?' He explains:

> It was *against* morality that my instinct turned with this questionable book, long ago; it was an instinct that aligned itself with life and that discovered for itself a fundamentally opposite doctrine and valuation of life – purely artistic and *anti-Christian* . . . I baptized it, not without taking some liberty – for who could claim to know the rightful name of the Antichrist? – in the name of a Greek god: I called it Dionysian.

An instinct that aligns itself with life – *purely artistic*. 'Dionysian,' I write again, and underline twice, in my notebook.

Art as solace

'Someone once said,' Maxine Kumin offers in her introduction to the poetry of Anne Sexton, 'that we possess art lest we perish of the truth.' She's quoting Nietzsche, of course, his famous aphorism about the purpose of art and the intolerable, nauseating absurdity of human existence. I love Kumin's dismissiveness here – *someone once said* – and suspect that this someone would have been both furious at being dismissed and also teeth-grindingly triumphant to be quoted by a twentieth-century American poet. Kumin uses the line as she reaches for ways to explain the inexplicable, to give voice to that which we struggle to articulate – the solace that Sexton found in poetry, the solace that arguably saved her from suicide, until it could no longer.

Clouds on the horizon

My son comes in one morning before seven, just after I have taken my photograph. He sits on my lap and reads with me. 'His wisdom is . . .' he whispers, reading the words aloud, forming them carefully and consciously. He slips on 'opium' and 'virtue' but does not ask me what they mean. 'Is it a poem, this book?' he asks me, curious. 'Yes, sort of,' I say. 'What's it about?' 'A man comes down from his cave in the mountains to tell the people what he has learned.' My son turns the book back to its front cover: a painting of a man on a mountain-top, looking towards a gleaming sun half-hidden by clouds on the horizon. 'They look weird, those clouds,' he decides. He slips off my lap and I look down, tired, to check the news before I get up to make breakfasts and clean dishes and prepare sandwiches. I see an article called 'Here comes the sun: Philosophy to help us in lockdown'. When I look up again, the moon is gone. I suppose it is behind the rainclouds that seem to be drifting across the sky. The dawn is over. The day begins. The storms are coming.

The abyss

It is not nearly as popular, or as quotable, but for me the most powerful image in Nietzsche's work of the relationship between art and despair comes from *The Birth of Tragedy*. Nietzsche presents the dark spots we see after looking at the sun as a kind of 'cure', and then goes on to offer us a sort of reverse vision of this phenomenon, the 'luminous spots' that might appear to 'cure eyes damaged by gruesome night'. Nietzsche claims that 'the poet's whole conception is nothing but precisely that bright image which healing nature projects before us after a glance into the abyss.'

I ask myself a lot of questions as I read. (The storms are coming.) Is it necessary for a poet to *glance into the abyss*? Is first light inspiring because it is always beautiful in a different way, because of its appearance – because it fills us with awe – or as a moment of reckoning before the day begins, as the end of night, as a compelling force? What does it mean, to *act*, to *articulate*?

I keep a sharp eye out for when Nietzsche speaks of poets, although he uses the terms 'poet', 'poetry' and 'poem' in ambiguous, nebulous and endearing ways ('we want to be the poets of our lives', is one example, from *The Joyous Science*). While art may be a necessary and vital response to the fundamental nihilism, pessimism, cynicism, absurdity, and despair of human life, Nietzsche seems to have a hard time settling on a position about poets. In *Zarathustra* the prophet speaks mournfully of poets and tries to avoid tackling a previous claim about poets being liars – liars because they work with language, liars because nothing they make is real, liars because they mask uncomfortable, nauseating reality, liars because they embellish, because of their dexterity with smoke and mirrors.

Zarathustra tries to deny, irritably, that he should be held to his previous opinions, but then goes on to speak scornfully of poets and their inadequacies. And yet Zarathustra is of course himself a poet, and ultimately, Nietzsche appears to conclude that although art and morality are both false and deceitful, art does not negate or condemn life. And so, Nietzsche continues to align himself with art and poetry as life-affirming, as possibility, as becoming, as potential.

Other words for 'dawn'

Elsewhere in Nietzsche, 'dawn' and 'tomorrow's morning' represent the possibility and opportunity for revaluation that is afforded to the poet-philosophers of the future, invigorated and liberated by the news that the 'old God is dead'. Dawn in French is *aube*, or *aurore*, in Latin, *aurora*. In Nietzsche's German, it is *dämmerung*, which is also the word for twilight. I think about this as I read *Zarathustra*, wondering how the translators know which one to select, whether it is always clear from the context which one Nietzsche is employing:

'But I am leaving you,' Zarathustra says. 'The time has come. Between dawn and dawn a new truth has come to me.'

Epilogue

The trees in the yard begin to blossom. They are *sakura*, Japanese cherry blossom, not fruit trees at all. They will not produce cherries, but are magnificently ornamental – an annual, ephemeral explosion of soft pink and snow white. They are all style – appearance alone. The petals drift down like snow when the children climb up into the branches to retrieve their football. The trees remind me of another life – of boulevards lined with blossom, of *hanami* picnics and shaved ice, of trains that cut through green valleys and forests of bamboo and mountains that erupt steeply out of the crowded cities and haughty graveyards. First light stops calling to me, or perhaps I no longer wish to listen. I stop rising with the dawn. The trees have spoken, and I have nothing left to say.

The Fertile Abyss

> The challenge, I thought and think, is to learn to use with freedom
> the cage we're shut up in. It's a painful contradiction: how can
> one use a cage with freedom . . .?
>
> — Elena Ferrante, *In the Margins*

CULLING

After the move I restock my bookshelves – how many books did
I calculate, again? Not many – barely enough to fill two large bookcases – and yet the boxes and boxes and boxes of books are almost
nauseating. I begin to cull. I could not cull before we moved – I had
to bring everything. I had to wrap myself up in all that I owned
because in the process of moving I was cold, exposed, and strangely
unweighted.

I cull brutally, systematically. All the books I read for my honours
thesis about suicide terrorism. All the biographies of Bob Dylan.
All the mediocre books by authors I otherwise love. I dedicate an

entire shelf to poetry and another to French texts. When I look at the restocked bookcases, I start to see something recognisable, something that seems to promise unity, cohesion. A coming together. Rather than a fragmented becoming, a hypothetical self, I see choices – dogged attempts at an impossible whole.

MISUNDERSTANDING

For Virginia Woolf, when we encounter a work of genius we experience an unnerving sense of recognition, as if a candle were being held up to what is already written on the walls of our mind:

> One holds every phrase, every scene to the light as one reads – for Nature seems, very oddly, to have provided us with an inner light by which to judge of the novelist's integrity or disintegrity. Or perhaps it is rather that Nature, in her most irrational mood, has traced in invisible ink on the walls of the mind a premonition which these great artists confirm; a sketch which only needs to be held to the fire of genius to become visible.

For Woolf this is an act of illumination – what was traced would not be legible without this light. Nietzsche's view of reading, and readers, is much dourer – we can only take from a text what we already know, he says. Nietzsche insists that his works will be misunderstood because the majority of those who encounter his work will not be able to understand the extent of his genius.

Like many people, I prefer Nietzsche's writings to other people's summaries or explanations of his concepts. So often, when reading the work of Nietzsche scholars, I have this niggling thought – 'that's not quite right' – 'they haven't quite grasped it' – knowing full well that I, myself, cannot claim to have a firm grip on anything. There's just some essence – some spirit – some scent, let's say, that you can smell but not describe, and can only, frowning, contemplate other attempts, whilst biting your pencil and deriding your own efforts. You can't sit down to write about being inspired by Nietzsche to revaluate your own values unless you're ready to accept that you're using his work to stage, or frame, your own encounter with yourself.

Accepting the potential that you are misunderstanding Nietzsche is, of course, just part of the fun. For some reason his accusation of poor readership reminds me of what I have been told is an old Hungarian expression: for a man with only a hammer in his toolbox, every problem looks like a nail.

For a woman with only Nietzsche in her toolbox, does every problem look like nihilism?

CLEARING OFF

I decide to write at the low table in our lounge room, sitting on the interlocking tatami mats we have bought for the new house. I have to clear the table before I begin. I move an enormous children's picture book called *Wild Cities*, two graphic novels, a book of crossword puzzles, a hard toy turtle, a cloth horse, a sketch book, a tin of 72 Derwent pencils, a wad of Blu Tack, a bottle of PVA glue, a colouring sheet with an uncoloured bouquet of flowers, a pen, a piece of paper with some pencil sketches of a snake, a brontosaurus, and a flying spider. I also move a small round dish that contains hundreds of tiny plastic mosaic pieces; a piece of paper that has a tally of 'Could Find' and 'Couldn't Find' (one mark for 'Could Find', five for 'Couldn't'), and a nonfiction book about the universe. It strikes me that I should clean the table before I begin to work, and I am surprised at how filthy it is. It seems to be covered in layers of grime that only become visible with a sponge and water. Finally, it is cleared, and cleaned, and I sit down to work.

CONFRONTATION

Because I am still struggling to read, I binge a series of lectures about Nietzsche from the Columbia Law School that are available on YouTube. In one of the early lectures, the scholar Jesús R. Velasco asks if we can use Nietzsche as a confrontation with ourselves in order to become something else, and I write this down along with all of the other variations of this question I have copied from scholars and from Nietzsche himself, all questions about the utility of Nietzsche, about becoming, about the value of confrontation and breaking apart in order to progress.

OVERHEARD

My son has lost a precious rock that he bought minutes before, dropping it into the Murray River from the jetty at Goolwa. We are at the end of a short trip we have taken with my in-laws, who have finally received special dispensation to come from France after years of waiting for travel restrictions to ease. 'It's good,' I tell my husband as we sit at a distillery on the edge of the river. 'It's a good lesson in regret.' As I say this, I overhear my mother-in-law as she cuddles my son on her lap. 'Si tu arrêtes de me dire que j'ai un gros cul,' *If you stop telling me I've got a fat bum*, 'Si tu arrêtes de me dire que j'ai le cou d'un dindon,' *If you stop telling me I have the neck of a turkey*, 'et les oreilles qui balancent,' *and earlobes that swing*, 'Je vais t'acheter un autre bijoux,' *I will buy you another jewel*, she says. 'Vraiment? *Really?* My son's eyes light up and my husband rolls his at me. So much for the lesson in regret. 'He never says those things,' I grumble. She laughs and pats me on the arm.

POETS

To the question: How do authors of sketches, stories, and novels get along in life, the following answer can or must be given: They are stragglers and they are down at heel.

– Robert Walser, 'Poets'

ORIGINS

Once, at a night class in Beginner's Spanish, I was asked to complete a family tree, and although this must have seemed like a primary school-level task, I did not know what to do with the branches and spaces above my grandparents. My Spanish teacher gestured at the empty spaces, asking '¿Y los otros?' and I shrugged, not yet knowing the words *adoptada, repudiado, huérfana*. Adopted, disowned, orphaned. 'Los otros no lo sé,' I tried. *The others I do not know.* Her frown deepened. My extended family had crossed oceans, and the importance of lineage had splintered and fragmented somewhere along the journey. I could tell the teacher was perplexed, but I did not have the language to explain further.

MARGINALIA

In my copy of *The Lonely City* by Olivia Laing I have scrawled the following in the margins:

Fragmentation: <u>in dialogue with</u> the will to cohesion, the uniting of fragments, or disparate, even competing elements, into one recognisable whole. Not just in literature. In terms of the project of our own selves, our own lives. The human instinct to bring or knit things together into a meaningful whole.

DEMOLITION

The demolition of our old house is surprisingly orderly, even elegant. The tiles of the roof are removed, along with the windowpanes and the doors, exposing the original wooden roof frame, the beams, the struts, and rafters. The carpets are then torn up. The back rooms, the bedrooms, toilet, and bathroom, are demolished first. It is a very deliberate stripping, a careful deconstruction. This is a job, after all, to take a building apart, door by door, brick by brick. It is nothing like what I had imagined – a wrecking ball swinging wildly, fracturing home and memory, the destruction of something dear and fragile, like a child stomping on a grasshopper. Instead, it is the work of a conscientious biologist, each limb removed with tweezers and labelled carefully under plate glass.

It is not as tidy as that, of course, but the demolition takes many weeks, section by section. It is not a catastrophe. It is an unpacking, a reversal. It reminds me of Bob's job, to remove the invasive species, to return a site to its native state. 'I'm not really a gardener,' he said one day after I introduced him as such. 'I spend most of my time killing stuff.'

When I go to take photographs of the deconstruction of our old house there is only one man working, clearing away pieces of rubble by hand. The back area is strewn with bricks and beams, the concrete foundation of the house now exposed. The front of the house is still standing, the familiar façade of our old home with its plate of stained glass next to the white front door still intact. The garden is overgrown but undamaged – the *Salvia leucantha* is nearly my height now, a wild hedge of purple and sage green. 'I planted that salvia!'

I inform the man proudly. 'Still going strong,' he replies, nodding. He is uncomfortable with me taking photographs – I should not have mentioned that I am a writer, that I am writing about the house being demolished. He thinks I am a journalist. He does not realise I am a poet, that I am not writing a bitter opinion piece about development, but rather, as an act of my own deconstruction.

OVERHEARD (PART II)

'Do you want,' I hear my son ask my daughter at dinner, 'a goat that speaks French?' She shrugs in response and he continues, 'I do. I think it would be good, for Maman's language.'

POETS (PART II)

If, again, it is asked: How and where, i.e., in what sorts of dwelling do writers mostly live?, the answer is very simply this: It is a fact that they prefer to live, often, in attics, high up, with views all around, because from there they enjoy the broadest and freest outlook upon the world. They also like, as is well known, to be independent and unconstrained. Let us hope that they pay the rent, sometimes, as punctually as possible.

– Robert Walser, 'Poets'

DREAMS

I dreamed that I was trying to find out Heidegger's first name. It begins, I said, with an 'A', and proceeded to mouth 'Anaïs', 'Antigone', 'Ariadne', but was interrupted (as all dreamers are) by one seduction

126

or another, clinging to my quest in bursts. Do you know, I asked a figure standing over me in a field, the name, the first name of the philosopher Heidegger? And later, clinging to a raft on bracing seas, asking the group next to me between waves, Heidegger – do you know – his first name? Finally, in the arms of a lover between the sheets, laughing off her earnest declarations and tearful proposals and turning serious: But actually, I do have an important question: could you tell me, would you happen to remember, the first name of the German philosopher *Heidegger* . . . ?

REVALUATION (PART IV)

A revaluation of all values, this question-mark so black, so huge it casts a shadow over him who sets it up – such a destiny of a task compels one every instant to run out into the sunshine so as to shake off a seriousness grown all too oppressive.

– Nietzsche, 'Foreword', *Twilight of the Idols*

DEMOLITION (PART II)

In front of the defiant swathe of salvia is a pile of bricks, the bathtub full of electrical cables and the bathroom sink lying on its side. Perched on some bricks is a small excavator, as colourful as a toy, aquamarine with a lime green cab. Looking back at the photos I took of the demolition, I notice what is still intact: the tiles around the sink, the slate blue laundry floor. The kitchen is full of rubble and as I zoom in and recognise the motifs and details of our previous life, I have a jolt of claustrophobia. Even with the roof removed and the blue sky winking behind the wooden beams, *It's too small*, my heart shrieks. *We cannot go back there! Don't make us go back there!*

THE ABYSS

My research on nihilism leads me into the abyss. That sounds like a metaphor for having a nervous breakdown, but actually it's a theoretical move. Or perhaps it's a poetical move – it's true, I like the sound of it, *the abyss*. Nietzsche uses it often. In *Thus Spoke Zarathustra*, it is the abyss over which the tightrope walker is suspended. The abyss is treacherous, suffocating. Nietzsche warns that in the abyss, 'the glance plunges *downward* and the hand grasps *upward*. There the heart grows giddy through its two-fold will'. For Zarathustra, the inverse is true: he must steel himself against his instinct to glance upwards towards the heights whilst also trying to hold onto the depths. Either way, Nietzsche describes the soul as torn between two states – glancing, and gripping. What are we looking at, and what are we holding onto?

MONOLOGUE

One day I realise the children are asking less of me; our conversations have become more one-sided. They are able to carry more, and they do, recognising that I like to listen.

'When I am older,' my son says, 'I would like to have a house in the hills. Next to a river. With a pet goat, and a carpet python and a cat with black and orange stripes that looks like a tiger. And in winter they will all wear a little beanie and a jumper, and in spring they will wear t-shirts and hats. And in summer, they will wear a singlet and a hat that is big, that goes around like this, with a big wide bit around the top. And in autumn they will wear a long-sleeve shirt and a beret. Except for the python. The python will not have the jumper, or the t-shirt, or the singlet, or the long-sleeve. But they will all wear, what's it called? That long bit that hangs down from the neck? A tie. They will all wear ties every day, even the python.'

THE ABYSS (PART II)

Heidegger links the abyss to poetic duty. The poet, 'sooner than other mortals and otherwise than they', must 'reach into the abyss' in order to *know and understand* the abyss. I start to think that the way out of my stuckness – my going-and-not-going – might involve descent, a sort of sinking, submerging. I am less interested in what the abyss *is* or what the abyss *means* than in how I might progress into it, how I might claw and scratch and grind a way out of (or do I mean into?) this impasse.

MEANING (PART IV)

A story means, at the highest level, not by what it concludes but by how it proceeds.

– George Saunders, *A Swim in a Pond in the Rain*

DESTITUTE TIMES

In Heidegger's essay 'What are Poets For?', the main thesis hinges on the idea of the duty of a poet in *destitute times*. How is Rainer Maria Rilke's poetry, Heidegger asks, related to the destitution of time? 'How deeply does it reach into the abyss?' *Destitute times*, of course, are the result of the death of God – they are nihilistic times. I should follow this track into the abyss to try to unpick how Heidegger, following Nietzsche, understands the role of poetry in response to the nihilism of modernity, but instead I become obsessed with this phrase, *destitute times*. I cannot explain why. I don't know if I'm avoiding something or on the right track. If I've veered off course or finally picked up the scent. My obsession with the term *destitute times* has something to do with the way language works, with translation, with my vested interest in Heidegger's question of where the poet can get to, within the abyss, assuming the poet goes where the poet can go. I spend hours hunting for the original German, trying to find the poem by Friedrich Hölderlin from which Heidegger takes the phrase, considering various translations and etymology until I begin to wonder if this quest, itself, is a sort of abyss.

DOVE MI TROVO

Months before she sets fire to her life and leaves her husband, a friend tells me I should read Jhumpa Lahiri's *Dove mi trovo*, translated into English as *Whereabouts*. We are skiving off, stopped at the lights with the windows down, wearing black swimsuits and sweltering in the summer heat. I wave my hand dismissively, telling her I have too much to read, but she insists in a strange, distant sort of way, and the faraway sound of her voice impresses me. She seems oddly enchanted, and I, too, want to be enchanted.

The book, composed in Italian, is a series of vignettes in which a deeply solitary woman moves through a deeply solitary life in Rome. A seductive narrative for overworked mothers living through a pandemic. As I read, I wonder if Lahiri composing in her non-native Italian has something to do with the intoxicating aloneness of the narrative, if she has accessed, via this foreign language, a peculiarly remote elsewhere somewhere deep within.

Later, when my friend's soon-to-be-ex-husband is trying to locate when and how he lost her, he texts me to ask if there are any books that *might help me to understand who she is, in this moment.* I immediately think about recommending Lahiri's book to him, but I don't, instead sending him a list of books that might help him process his grief. I keep *Dove mi trovo* as a place in which she cannot be found, cannot be located.

DESTITUTE TIMES (PART II)

Heidegger's use of the phrase 'destitute times' comes from Hölderlin's elegy 'Bread and Wine'. Heidegger takes the central question of 'What Are Poets For?' from Hölderlin's poem, quoting, *'and what are poets for in a destitute time?'* I go hunting for the original German, a language I do not know. Heidegger's essay, in German, is *Wozu Dichter?* and I find a version that offers the original German citation of Hölderlin: 'und wozu Dichter in dürftiger Zeit?' The word I seem to be looking for – *dürftiger –* is blurry, the copy I have is poor – the website I am using calls itself 'World Documents'. I autotranslate it into English to check my spelling. *Poorer, meagre, scanty, sparse,* the machine tells me.

I want to search the German text of *Wozu Dichter?* for Heidegger's repetition of *dürftiger,* which, in the English translation as 'destitute', crops up continually (along with 'abyss' and 'venture'). I cannot find a less blurry version of the text than this dubious 'World Documents' website. I copy some of the text into an actual Word document and the result is disappointing (poor, meagre, scanty, sparse), and riddled with errors:

> . . . und wozu Dichter in drftiger Zeit?' frgt Hlderlins Elegie
> B r o d und Wein'. Wir verstehen heute kaum die Frage.

Frgt is not a word, Hölderlin is misspelled, Brod has been peculiarly spaced out. The word *dürftiger* has also been mangled, making it impossible to search for. I text a friend with a German husband. *Ask Olaf,* I type, *how he would translate 'dürftiger Zeit'.*

I get no reply.

The Abyss (Part III)

Rilke, according to Heidegger, differentiates between *Urgrund*, Nature, and *Abgrund*, abyss. Nature is pristine, surface – the abyss is soil, ground, a tending downwards. Again, I wonder: if we are all, for the time being, *grounded*, is there value in turning our gaze from the skies and looking not just at what surrounds us, but also considering a more fertile turn inwards? Can we tend downwards, for a time?

The Overworked Poets Society

I am aware that it's a failure of this work, written during a pandemic by a woman in precarious employment and housing with two young children and anxious in-laws who don't speak English and a spouse who is unexpectedly classed as an essential worker (called upon to coordinate the translation of urgent health announcements into dozens of languages), that I don't adequately show what that looks like. I know I'm not demonstrating how overworked I am, how much pressure I am under. I just don't want to. I just *don't want to*. Imagine doing all that labour, and then doing the double work of *explaining* all that labour.

Madame Pumpernickel

The fact that my mother does not speak French did not stop her from composing a short nursery rhyme in French about an imaginary woman called Madame Pumpernickel using the Berlitz French phrase book she had carried during her travels through Europe in her twenties ('in an old beat-up Fiat', she tells me). It begins:

'Bonjour, Madame Pumpernickel, comment allez-vous aujourd'hui?'
We learned to recite it as kids, copying her gleefully poor pronunciation and embarrassing ourselves in front of French-speakers. The
final line, 'Mais je departerais!', *But I would leave!*, doesn't even make
sense. It makes me laugh to think of it now – I picture our house in
Queensland with the wooden bead curtains and mounted ferns, the
view from our balcony over the rainforest to the ocean, Mum in a
bikini collecting the ripe mangoes from the tree in the backyard to
make ice cream. I think of her composing in a foreign language to
pass the time, to remind her of travels, of the world out there. But
there's a sadness to it, too, a young mother making her own nursery
rhymes from a random phrase book because she had not been raised
with any of her own to pass on, a motherless mother inventing ways
to parent in a tropical paradise.

DESTITUTE TIMES (PART III)

I know the philosophers I'm looking at are famously difficult and
controversial. Nietzsche with his bombastic, backflipping tenden-
cies, his scorn. Heidegger with his awful personality, his abhorrent
fascism, as well as his convoluted prose. I wish I could say I'm reading
their work because I feel obligated, but it's not true. I'm in the work
because it feels necessary. Not because I admire them as people, or
because I approve of all of their ideas, but because I'm drawn in, as if
by a gravitational pull, to what I feel is evidence of a creative inquiry
that verges on madness, an almost impossible quest into the meaning
of the abyss. I'm interested in the language that can been wrested
out of that search, what emerges as a result of that enquiry. There
is something thrilling about the words that Heidegger advocates as
a response to the destitutions of our times. Words like, 'flinging
loose' and 'release' – words that sound like terrible (and thus sacred)

risk, like the opposite of being stuck, of being grounded. I look up synonyms for 'venture':

travel – journey – go – move – proceed – progress – set out – set forth – rove – wander – stray – drift – migrate – advance – ventilate

Ventilate! 'If that which has been flung were to remain out of danger, it would not have been ventured,' I copy carefully in pencil into my notebook. *The ventured is unprotected but the venture is its security.*

INWARD

After *Dove mi trovo* I start to read about Lahiri's move into Italian. She began studying Italian seriously in her late thirties, about the age I am now, motivated by a passion for the language rather than circumstance or location. Lahiri writes about her relationship with Italian in the book *In Other Words*, which is published as a bilingual text, Ann Goldstein's English translation facing Lahiri's original Italian. I find the book astonishingly sensual. Lahiri writes of going into a foreign language as going into the woods, going inward, slowly and hesitantly. She writes of language as bone and marrow, as a quest that is constantly thwarted. She describes her frustration, the feeling that she is skirting the boundaries, unable to reach the heart of Italian as its internal, hidden layers elude her.

BREAKING

According to friends and acquaintances, at the end of his life Heidegger repeated the words, *Nietzsche hat mich kaputt gemacht*. 'Nietzsche broke me'. It sounds like a lament, and maybe it was.

But to be broken open, to be broken apart, in order to go beyond, is also very Nietzschean. Did Heidegger get beyond the breaking? Is there a point beyond the breaking?

SOMEWHERE ELSE

Over the years Venice has had an increasingly unsettling impact on me. Its devastating beauty pierces me, I'm overwhelmed by the fragility of life . . . Crossing the bridges again and again makes me think of the passage that we all make on the earth, between birth and death. Sometimes, crossing certain bridges, I fear I've already reached the beyond.

When I write in Italian, I feel the same disquiet, in spite of my love for the language. The step that I'm taking seems like a leap into the void, an inversion of myself . . . Yet both in Venice and on the page, bridges are the only way to move into a new dimension, to get past English, to arrive somewhere else.

– Jhumpa Lahiri, *In Other Words*

MARINE LOVER

The French poet-philosopher Luce Irigaray was expelled from her college after the publication of her second doctoral thesis, *Speculum of the Other Woman*, a radical feminist interrogation of phallocentrism in classical works of philosophy and psychoanalysis. Irigaray said that she wrote the book 'not in a library or at a desk, but in the woods or by the sea'. In her later book *Marine Lover*, Irigaray speaks in an intimate address to Nietzsche's Zarathustra, using the more intimate pronoun *tu* instead of the formal *vous*, speaking to him (and with him) as her equal. Irigaray later claimed the entire book was written in dialogue with a Nietzsche with whom she considered herself to be romantically entangled ('Ce n'est pas un livre *sur* Nietzsche mais *avec* Nietzsche qui est pour moi un partenaire amoureux' – *It's not a book* about *Nietzsche, but a book* with *Nietzsche, who is, for me, a lover*). Despite her affection for him, *Marine Lover* also grapples with Irigaray's concern that Zarathustra/Nietzsche might not be good for her:

> And yet I still love you too well in my silence to remember the movement of my own becoming . . . You have always trapped me in your web.

Irigaray also rebukes Nietzsche for what she considers his most 'abysmal thought', the concept of 'eternal recurrence', as a philosophy that denies and repudiates the idea of origin, and thus the idea of *maternal* origin:

> And isn't it by forgetting the first waters that you achieve immersion in your abysses and the giddy flight of one who wings far away, perched at such heights that no sap rises there and no thread secures his way?

Ah, but Luce, I think. Do you not know what some mothers know, mothers raised without mothers, mothers who were raised by motherless mothers? That sap *does not necessarily rise*, that thread *does not necessarily secure*?

DEMOLITION (PART II)

As a writer I can demolish myself, I can reconstruct myself. I can join words together and work on sentences without ever being considered an expert. I'm bound to fail when I write in Italian, but, unlike my sense of failure in the past, this doesn't torment or grieve me.

– Jhumpa Lahiri, 'Teach Yourself Italian'

Demolition and reconstruction and failure and escape. *Demolition* and *reconstruction* and *failure* and *escape*.

THE PIG SONG

Pigs, pigs, up and down!
They do what they do.
Pigs, pigs, up and down!
You can eat them, too.

My son rocks around the house singing his latest composition. I write it down and stick it on the fridge, referring to it as his poem. His eyes grow wide. 'Is it really a *poem*?' he asks, awed.

DESTITUTE TIMES (PART IV)

A different translation of Hölderlin's poem offers the phrase *dürftiger Zeit* as 'lean years':

. . . In the meantime, however, often I think that
It might be better to sleep than to be so bereft,
So endlessly waiting. And what's there to say or to do?
What's the use, in lean years, of a poet? I don't know.

– Hölderlin, 'Bread and Wine'

I like the surrounding text, too – 'it might be better to sleep than to be so bereft / So endlessly waiting.' 'Lean years' is an elegant version of 'destitute times', and far better than other translations I find that offer it as 'empty years', or worse, 'in times of need'. But it is the term *destitute* I am strangely obsessed with. I suspect *dürftiger* has been translated as 'destitute' in the translation of Heidegger's essay because whatever word is used must have a certain mutability in order to withstand the demands Heidegger makes of this term, as in the following:

> Long is the destitute time of the world's night . . . At this night's midnight, the destitution of the time is greatest. Then the destitute time is no longer able even to experience its own destitution. That inability, by which even the destitution of the destitute state is obscured, is the time's absolutely destitute character.

INWARD (PART II)

Lahiri describes unknown words in Italian as a 'dizzying yet fertile abyss'. There it is again, *the abyss*. I had never thought of the abyss as *fertile*, but when I think about Heidegger's discussion of Rilke's *Abgrund*, the earthiness, the soiliness, it seems possible.

Reading Lahiri, I consider what it might mean to sink into the abyss as a conscious choice, if the abyss is both terrifying and also full of radical potential, as Nietzsche and Heidegger and Irigaray and others would have it. Sinking down, sinking deep, into watery depths. Instead of travelling, leaving, looking outward, reaching beyond, attempting to leap over, out of – could I perhaps go inward, and sink into *the fertile abyss* of my own self?

Marine Lover

Lower than the earth's crust you must now descend to announce the way of the earth. Remind yourself that all that happens beneath ensures the progress of your beyond. And know that a solid plane is never more than a solid plane. That it is based upon life underground, life underwater, fires and winds, all covered by it but which, under this mantle, move without cease.

– Luce Irigaray, *Marine Lover*

Unravelling

For weeks I carry an old piece of torn fabric around with me, trying to find time to write about it. It distresses me – both the fabric being torn, and not being able to write about it. I have it wrapped around a copy of *The Wind in the Willows*, which I am also trying, and failing, to find time to write about. I carry the book wrapped in fabric like a parcel I never have time to post.

The fabric is a ribbed navy-blue cotton singlet with pencil-thin white stripes that I bought at the Japanese chain store Muji one afternoon in the train station of Hirakata. I bought four singlets at the same time: white with black stripes, charcoal grey, mustard yellow, and this one. The navy blue was my favourite and thus the one that has become so threadbare that it is, now, unwearable, pock-marked in places – an archipelago of holes across the back where it hung on the clothesline, under the arms, near the neckline. Even as I touch it now, I want to wear it – it feels so soft and loose and appealing.

In general I am a minimalist, but I cling to the singlet because I can feel my connection to Japan fraying. My memories are fading. I am no longer someone who has just returned from living in Japan. The clothes I bought there – the clothes I bought because I needed them, not as mementos or souvenirs – are starting to disintegrate. I am losing, very kinaesthetically, very tangibly, contact with the life I led in Japan, the life that had me rushing to Muji after work to stock up on singlets because I had not expected, was not sartorially prepared for, the sticky, humid summer.

DESTITUTE TIMES (PART V)

The world, writes Heidegger, is so destitute that it has no awareness – cannot experience – its own destitution. 'The destitution is wholly obscured,' he states, 'in that it now appears as nothing more than the need that wants to be met.' Working backwards from that – presuming we accept the world is destitute – must we then identify the *need that wants to be met*? Is this the yearning within us that we find hard to allocate? We cannot meet that need (that is not the project), but is the task in part to articulate it, to say this, *this* is the need? To commit ourselves to being aware of our lack of awareness of the destitution of the world? Is that why I decided to spend so much time reading Nietzsche? Are there answers for me here? I struggle to believe it.

INWARD (PART III)

To get inward I find I must visit a lot of forests and take a lot of hikes and trek down to a lot of coves and waterfalls in places that have no mobile reception. On these trips I am often morose; the descent feels unnatural. I snack on dried fruit and nuts, the children holler to each other about crabs in rockpools, we stack wood to make campfires, the air smells like eucalypt and ocean and the sky is full of shooting stars and still I feel like the journey inwards is a necessary evil, forced upon me by the difficult circumstances, something I would have preferred, if I could, to avoid altogether.

WAYFARERS ALL

The children begin to debate what books I read to them in the evening. I want to enjoy the reading, too – I want poetry, they want plot and adventure. We compromise on classic adventure stories. Sometimes I am too ambitious, and we have to quit because my son finds the language too difficult to understand. He has a particular growl he uses to tell me I'm asking too much of him, that I am ruining bedtime, his favourite time of day.

We have a proper battle over Kenneth Grahame's *The Wind in the Willows*. I try to convince him to let the lengthy descriptions of the seasons and the river wash over him so he can enjoy the adventures of Badger, Rat, Mole and Toad. He is appeased by the funny dialogue and the outrageous Toad and lets me continue until we hit the chapter 'Wayfarers All'. The chapter begins, 'The Water Rat was restless, and he did not exactly know why'.

As the Water Rat watches the other animals prepare for their regular migratory voyage south for the winter, he begins to feel uneasy. Grahame explains that the Water Rat is 'a self-sufficing animal, rooted to the land, and whoever went, he stayed; still, he could not help noticing what was in the air, and feeling some of its influence in his bones.' The chapter is rich in description of the changing of the seasons and the Water Rat's sudden and debilitating *Fernweh*. Rat, too, is stuck. What will he do, in the face of this unaccustomed restlessness? I feel a quiver in myself as I read. I lay my hand on my son's chest and insist that he quiet his growl. I tell him he can stare at the ceiling and feel confused if he wants, if he could please just stop interrupting me.

DESTITUTE TIMES (PART VI)

Heidegger is capable of passages of fierce poetics in the face of despair that rival any of Nietzsche's:

> Yet we must think of the world's night as a destiny that takes place this side of pessimism and optimism. Perhaps the world's night is now approaching its midnight. Perhaps the world's time is now becoming the completely destitute time. But also perhaps not, not yet, not even yet, despite the immeasurable need, despite all suffering, despite nameless sorrow, despite the growing and spreading peacelessness, despite the mounting confusion. Long is the time because even terror, taken by itself as a ground for turning, is powerless as long as there is no turn with mortal men. But there is a turn with mortals when these find the way to their own nature. That nature lies in this, that mortals reach into the abyss sooner than the heavenly powers.

Don't ask me if this has any philosophical value: I am beginning to think that I have given up on philosophy.

DOVE MI TROVO (PART II)

The friend who has left her husband – the friend in the black swimsuit who recommended Lahiri's *Dove mi trovo* – is also the friend that lent me *The Wind in the Willows*, a hardcover version illustrated by Roberta Carter Clark. My friend's departure from her marriage is a shock to everyone except me: I have watched her drowning for years, trying to suppress her instinct to flee because of the children. One day she just does it, seemingly without warning – furiously rising up and gulping at the air.

*

Her husband is distraught, blindsided, dissatisfied with my book recommendations. He asks to talk to me about it, as the 'person who knows her best in this moment', and I arrive at their home one evening prepared to be both gentle and honest. I tell him that there is nothing he can do, there is no way he can improve himself, be a better spouse, win her back. It's not that she wants him to be different, to be better. She doesn't want another partner. She doesn't want a different type of marriage. 'She wants to be alone,' I tell him. 'You can't compete with alone. You can't make yourself more like nothing.'

Unravelling (Part II)

Of course, I am also attempting to hold onto the Japanese singlet – to not discard it – by writing about it. I am so distressed by all of this fraying, by my increasingly tattered connection with *ailleurs*, elsewhere, that I try to restitch it back into my life through words.

Now that vaccines are readily available, travel restrictions are easing, and one of my Japanese students moves to Adelaide to study. He comes to our house one Sunday to visit. I try to find a photo album from our time in Japan to show him, but I have misplaced it in the move and this, like the disintegration of my favourite singlet, seems horribly befitting.

My student gives me a small cloth as a gift. It is orange and green with a repeating motif of the famous deer that populate his hometown in Nara. I'm not sure if it is a dishcloth or a placemat and I look up the website on the packaging instead of asking him because I do not want to embarrass either of us. I cannot find the cloth on the website, but instead find myself mesmerised by pages of linen bedding and pyjama sets. There is a small image at the bottom of one page that shows a woman in a crumpled bed holding a book she has nearly finished, sunlight falling across the bedsheets. In bed, during the day, reading, dressed in luxurious fabrics. I find myself thinking of it long after I have closed the webpage. I go back to the site later in the day but although I try for some time, I cannot relocate the image.

In the months that follow, my Japanese clothes all start to fray, and I get used to throwing them away, singlets, socks, blouses, t-shirts.

WAYFARERS ALL (PART II)

'First,' explain the swallows to Rat, who cannot understand why they must talk about leaving when it makes him feel so despondent, 'we feel it stirring within us, a sweet unrest; then back come the recollections one by one, like homing pigeons. They flutter through our dreams at night, they fly with us in our wheelings and circlings by day. We hunger to inquire of each other, to compare notes and assure ourselves that it was all really true, as one by one the scents and sounds and names of long-forgotten places come gradually back and beckon to us.'

REBELLION, STUPIDITY

Lahiri is eloquent about the pain and discomfort of wanting to speak a foreign language fluently. As she describes it: 'A stubborn attempt, a continuous trial.' It is desperately slow, in a way that feels unnatural, that goes against the internal wiring of the mind and body. Lahiri calls it disorienting, disquieting. It is a process that denies shortcuts, that refuses to be accelerated, that takes its own time, despite effort, despite commitment. Given it is so difficult, why, *why* persist? Lahiri calls it 'a transgression, a rebellion, an act of stupidity'.

I did not know, as a child, that my mother's nursery rhyme about Madame Pumpernickel was only the beginning of finding myself ridiculous in French. I began learning in earnest in a shabby youth hostel in London full of young French ex-pats who had moved to London to improve their English and instead found themselves working difficult, solitary jobs for minimum wage and sitting around in the evenings sharing sandwiches from Sainsburys for dinner. They adopted me in part because I did not speak French and was patient with their errors and their accents, and partly because talking to me allowed them to improve their English over bottles of absinthe and packets of cheap cigarettes.

I thought learning French would come to me easily, that I would immediately be impressive. Instead, when I began to use French, I discovered a new expression on the faces of my friends. The expression confused me: I could not immediately label it, as I might have been able to identify scorn, appreciation, intrigue, or disappointment. I began to watch for it in order to diagram it: a softening around the eyebrows, a tender smile. A kindly look. But something else – something stranger than affection, a sort of uncanny wistfulness. I tried to imagine when that expression might appear on my face – what feeling might trigger the same look – and realised with horror that my new friends were looking at me *as if I were adorable*. 'Je n'suis pas adorable,' I learned to snarl, *I am not adorable*, but it just made them chuckle. My closest friend, Nico, stopped making eye contact with me when I tried to speak in French because he could not control his reaction, and I could not control my defensiveness.

Being gazed at as if I were adorable was galling because when I spoke in French, I was my most daring and terrified self. I felt as if I was on stage in a jet-black leotard, sticking my head into a lion's mouth; to my friends I was merely parading in a small tutu, clomping my way through a ballet routine in front of the grown-ups. My French, which did not feel like a game, but like the most terrible and courageous twisting of my native state, my established patterns, was *amusing* to them, I was *adorable* to them.

It was hard to recover from this realisation.

THE ABYSS (PART IV)

It pleases me that the concept of *eternal recurrence* recurs, loops, returns, throughout Nietzsche's body of work:

> What if some day or night a demon were to steal after you into your loneliest loneliness and say to you: 'This life as you now live it and have lived it, you will have to live once more and innumerable times more; and there will be nothing new in it, but every pain and every joy and every thought and sigh and everything unutterably small or great in your life will have to return to you, all in the same succession and sequence . . . The eternal hourglass of existence is turned upside down again and again, and you with it, speck of dust!'

Nietzsche goes on to offer this as a test – would you curse the demon, and gnash your teeth, or would you answer, 'You are a god and never have I heard anything more divine'? Can you claim to love yourself, your life, and your fate to the extent that you desire every moment of your life 'once more and innumerable times more'?

In *Thus Spoke Zarathustra*, Zarathustra claims eternal recurrence as his most terrible and profound idea, and says it comes from *his abyss*; he explains it as his abyss *speaking*. He tells his friends that he has been spoken to by his *stillest hour*, a voiceless terror that assails him. Zarathustra weeps before this voice, afraid of what he must become. 'O, Zarathustra,' the voiceless abyss says, 'you shall go as a shadow of that which must come: thus you will command and commanding lead the way.' He answers, 'I am ashamed,' but the voiceless terror tells Zarathustra that he 'must yet become a child and without shame.'

Zarathustra is compelled to leave the Blissful Isles by the sudden realisation that he must fulfil his destiny elsewhere, under different conditions. On the journey away from his friends on the Blissful Isles, Zarathustra reflects on what motivated him to leave the joyful community he had founded there. It was a necessary and painful choice, and one he had not anticipated. 'I – did not hear: until at last my abyss stirred and my thought bit me,' he mourns.

WAYFARERS ALL (PART III)

The Rat . . . listened fascinated, and his heart burned within him. In himself, too, he knew that it was vibrating at last, that chord hitherto dormant and unsuspecting. The mere chatter of these southern-bound birds, their pale and second-hand reports, had yet power to awaken this wild new sensation and thrill him through and through with it . . . Today, to him gazing south with newborn need stirring in his heart, the clear sky over their long low outline seemed to pulsate with promise; today the unseen was everything, the unknown the only real fact of life.

– Kenneth Grahame, *The Wind in the Willows*

Rat finds himself yearning for adventures 'out there, beyond – beyond!' when he comes across a dusty wayfarer, the itinerant Sea Rat. The Sea Rat enchants the Rat with evocative tellings of his many adventures and voyages, encouraging the Rat to 'Take the Adventure, heed the call!' The Rat ends up packing his bags in a trance and preparing to leave forever when he is stopped by his friend, the Mole, who, fearing the Rat's glazed look and mechanical answers, physically restrains him. Rat tries to fight, then gives in and succumbs to a sort of hysterical sobbing before falling asleep. When he wakes he cannot explain what happened to him, and although he no longer wants to leave he is listless and dejected.

French

I think I would have quit trying to learn French if I hadn't met my husband – being clumsy and adorable was too much for my ego. Guillaume did not need me to speak French. He was already bilingual after spending most of his adult life in Australia. In fact, he was more comfortable in English. 'Do not,' his French friends warned me, 'let Guillaume teach you French. Il parle français comme un ado débile des années 80s.' *He speaks French like a dumb teenager from the 1980s.* But after our children were born, he spoke to them in French every day and learning French just became something that had to be done, like learning to be a mother.

FARNIENTE

I find myself compulsively reading Italian writer Elena Ferrante's Neapolitan Quartet, and then, as a result, all of Ferrante's essays on writing that have been translated into English. Falling in love with Ferrante's writing, which feels like a reckless swerve away from my research, is that delicious combination of illicit and idle; what the Italians call *farniente* – the pleasure of lazing around, sweet idleness.

The words 'idle' and 'lazy' have negative connotations – it's hard to think of a word in English like *farniente* that captures the bone-deep pleasure of dropping out. When Ferrante writes about writing, one feels she is reaching after something she cannot quite articulate – something like 'intentional madness', or 'drunk sobriety' – something not outside of a binary, but the result of crashing two opposing things against each other and considering the shards in the aftermath. It is not that I feel, particularly, that Ferrante has answers for me, but rather that reading her work sends me *elsewhere*, whatever that might mean, wherever that might be.

DREAMS (PART II)

I often dream in French, which for some is a marker of fluency. But lately when I dream in French, I find myself speaking in a rude, overdone English accent, accusing people of not taking me seriously. I stand with my hands on my hips, snarling at a man selling perfumes. 'Pourquoi tu me réponds en anglais quand je fais un effort de te parler en français?' *Why are you responding in English, when I am making the effort to speak in French?*

A JUMBLE OF FRAGMENTS

My mother left me a word in her dialect that she used to describe how she felt when she was racked by contradictory sensations that were tearing her apart. She said that inside her she had a *frantumaglia*, a jumble of fragments . . . It was the word for a disquiet not otherwise definable, it referred to a miscellaneous crowd of things in her head, debris in a muddy water of the brain. The *frantumaglia* was mysterious, it provoked mysterious actions, it was the source of all suffering not traceable to a single obvious cause. When she was no longer young, the *frantumaglia* woke her in the middle of the night, led her to talk to herself and then feel ashamed, suggested some indecipherable tune to sing under her breath that soon faded into a sigh, drove her suddenly out of the house, leaving the stove on, the sauce burning in the pot . . . The *frantumaglia* is the storehouse of time without the orderliness of history, a story.

— Elena Ferrante, *Frantumaglia*

WHAT MY FRENCH IS LIKE

At school pick-up one day, one of the other non-French-speaking parents asks me what my French is like. 'Yeah,' I reply nonsensically. 'I've been thinking about that myself.'

I never know how to answer. My French is pretty good for someone who began learning as an adult, but it's pretty poor for someone married to a Frenchman with two bilingual children.

Wayfarers All (Part IV)

The Rat cannot leave home, partly because the Mole refuses to let him march off under the spell of some seafaring raconteur, but also because leaving is simply not what the Rat does. So the Rat, full of longing, unable to follow the call, is stuck, at an impasse.

My son was, by this point in the chapter, muttering 'I don't get it' under his breath and making his throaty growling noise. 'I just don't understand what is HAPPENING,' he announces crossly one night. 'The Rat wants to leave to go on an adventure, but he can't,' I say. 'Why can't he?' 'Because the Mole has stopped him.' 'Why has the Mole stopped him?' 'Because the Rat was under a spell, the spell of the Seafaring Rat.' 'Did he use magic?' 'No, he used words, but words can be a type of magic.' 'So what is happening now?' 'The Mole is trying to cheer the Rat up, because he wanted to leave and have adventures, and now he cannot.' 'Why can't he?' 'I already told you, because the Mole stopped him. Just let me read now, there are only a few pages to go.' I place my hand gently on his chest and continue:

Casually then, and with seeming indifference, the Mole turned his talk to the harvest that was being gathered in, the towering wagons and their straining teams, the growing ricks, and the large moon rising over bare acres dotted with sheaves. He talked of the reddening apples around, of the browning nuts, of jams and preserves and the distilling of cordials; till by easy stages such as these he reached midwinter, its hearty joys and its snug home life, and then he became simply lyrical.

By degrees the Rat began to sit up and to join in. His dull eyes brightened, and he lost some of his listless air.

I am looking for answers now – this is the first one I lock away. Is it possible to turn longing, yearning, aching, for something unattainable – into *noticing*?

What My French Is Like (Part II)

Tell me what my French sounds like, I say to my husband. I tell him I want to be able to explain my French to an English-speaking audience. He plays me a clip of Tina Arena doing a TV interview in French. She answers (fluently, with an accent, making a stream of errors) a series of questions as she promotes her new album. 'I can't tell people I speak French like a multilingual soprano answering inane questions on morning TV,' I snap at him. He shrugs. 'That's what you sound like.'

Will to Cohesion

And it is all my art and aim to compose into one and bring together what is fragment and riddle and dreadful chance . . .

    To redeem the past and to transform every 'it was' into an 'I wanted it thus!' – that alone I would call redemption.

             – Nietzsche, *Thus Spoke Zarathustra*

Shame

I still remember the sticky, awkward early years of learning French. I remember throwing a box of tissues at my husband in frustration when he laughingly corrected my pronunciation. I remember confusing the words *bête*, meaning beast, and *bite*, which is slang for cock, while talking to a friend about the film *Beauty and the Beast* as we walked around the city of Tours. My friend laughed so hard she had to stop walking, wiping tears from her eyes, gasping that *La Belle et La Bite* would be a good title for a porno.

BELLE-MÈRE

In French the word for mother-in-law is *belle-mère*, meaning 'beautiful mother', and it is also the term for stepmother. Because of our divorced and remarried families, I have three *belles-mères* – a step-mother, and two mothers-in-law. The one I write about here is my husband's mother, Mamie Solange. Solange is the first French person I love whose English is worse than my French.

Même maintenant j'ai du mal à écrire d'elle sans utiliser le français. Even now I struggle to write about Solange without using French. *On existe, Solange et moi, en français.* Solange and I – we exist in French.

Solange loves my children with a primal, inexhaustible ferocity that still shocks me. Before they were born, we chatted politely but afterwards we spoke for hours out of necessity: Solange wanted to know about every tooth and every rash and every whimper. My devotion to my babies did not blind me to how dull they were, how desperately mundane their development, and I made a concentrated effort not to bore my friends and family. But Solange was as interested as I was. Solange put up with my wonky French and my mistakes because I was talking to her about her beloved grandchildren and I pushed through my shame because she was the perfect audience, because she too found these ordinary little creatures endlessly fascinating.

How to Use a Cage with Freedom

Maintain distance: yes, but only to then get as close as possible. Avoid the pure outburst? Yes, but then burst out. Aim at consistency? Yes, but then be inconsistent. Make a polished, highly polished, draft, until the words no longer encounter friction with the meanings? Yes, but then leave it rough. Overload the genres with conventional expectations? Yes, but in order to disappoint them. That is, inhabit the forms and then deform everything that doesn't contain us entirely, that can't in any way contain us.

— Elena Ferrante, *In the Margins*

French (Part II)

So my French muscle strengthened quickly, in chatting to Solange, but not universally. Imagine biceps that can only carry the objects they have been trained to carry: domestic items, nursery rhymes, children's belongings. I never used the subjunctive, or the literary past tense. I spoke directly, subjectively, my arms full of *biberons, couches, peluches* (bottles, nappies, stuffed toys), my days full of *dodo, lolo, bêtises* (naps, milk, naughtiness).

Misheard

At the end of one of our regular camping trips we have lunch in a stringybark forest in what feels like the innermost wintery heart of a national park. We drive up to a bluff to find some toilets and I get tired of watching the surly kangaroos on the bluff (dismissive, scornful creatures) while waiting for the children, so I ask my husband for the keys to the car. I am scratching the earth with my toe and mumbling, perhaps, looking the way I look sometimes, which is to say, surly and despondent. He comes and gives me a kiss. We stare at each other for a long moment. 'Now can I have the keys?' I ask, and he shouts with laughter. 'Oh!' he exclaims. 'You said *keys*.'

THE MOON

After years of exposure, I've developed a sort of shamelessness in my French. I've hit a plateau of adequate functionality; I've built up my resilience so that I feel no embarrassment about my clawings, gropings for words or my blatantly poor expression. I am not motivated to improve. As the French say, *ça va*. It goes. I am recalcitrant – resistant to improving, to improvement. 'I think for you,' my French nephew says, 'your main problem is that you confuse your feminine and masculine, you do not know the gender of nouns.' 'I think my main problem,' I reply, 'is that I do not care, it doesn't matter to me. I say *le lune*, I say *la lune*, it makes no difference, you know I mean the moon.' He laughs, uneasy, and I can tell I have not convinced him. *Le lune* is not, for him, the moon.

THE ARENA OF THE UNWELL

The female writer must prove 'by summoning, beckoning and getting together that she was not a skimmer of surfaces merely, but had looked beneath into the depths', says Virginia Woolf. I have been skimming the surface. I have been scattered; resistant; unwell; *in pieces*. The truth is that I do not believe in wholes, in unity, in absolutes. Who could? But I begin to see that perhaps the answer is *nobody*, and that cohesion, like meaning, could be something that we seek, something that we *actively work towards*, even if we come at it from a place of profound disbelief.

Debilitating illnesses gave Beckett and Nietzsche a sense of incapacitation, and I wonder if these experiences brought the investigation of mortality and meaning closer to them – if their various maladies made them feel closer to death, and thus also life.

Will to Cohesion (Part II)

Over time, writing has come to mean giving shape to a permanent balancing and unbalancing of myself, arranging fragments in a frame and waiting to mix them up.

– Elena Ferrante, *In the Margins*

What My French Is Like (Part III)

There's a story about my grandma learning to drive. She had to drive in a straight line, following the tram tracks that lead from the city to the beach. That's it – that's all she had to do to get her driver's licence. Once, in a supermarket carpark, she came back to the car to find it boxed in by other vehicles and she had to ask someone else to reverse it out, because she had never learned how.

This is also what my French is like.

INTENTIONS

On beginning to keep a diary, Virginia Woolf laid out her intentions. She wanted to keep a record that was

> loose-knit and yet not slovenly, so elastic that it will embrace anything, solemn, slight or beautiful, that comes into my mind. I should like it to resemble some deep old desk or capacious hold-all, in which one flings a mass of odds and ends without looking them through. I should like to come back, after a year or two, and find that the collection had sorted itself and refined itself and coalesced, as such deposits so mysteriously do, into a mould, transparent enough to reflect the light of our life, and yet steady, tranquil compounds with the aloofness of a work of art . . .

This kind of writing takes a degree of faith that I do not always have. In response to this lack of faith I think *I must just keep pocketing things*. Woolf was a hoarder, famously messy. I think of creative types like this, surrounded by mess, hundreds of little trinkets that they save for inspiration. As if a muse is something external, a little kleptomaniac filling space with junk.

WILL TO COHESION (PART III)

On my desk I have two wooden shards from a giant eucalyptus that fell during a recent storm. The huge, splintered tree lay across the path of my hike, and I was surprised at how thick the shards were, how clearly delineated. They seemed possible only as the result of this massive storm, this terrible shattering. The shards fit neatly into my pocket, and I carried them home, partly to use them to think about fracture, and fragment, and wholeness, and unity, and cohesion, but also because I found them beautiful.

FORMS OF ADDRESS

At a training session for volunteers who want to be on radio, Guillaume tells the group that when he writes his radio scripts, he likes to address the listener directly – the listener singular, rather than the listening audience en masse, *tu* rather than *vous*. This cannot be distinguished in English, of course, in the way he addresses his audience – you is you is you. He's describing the way he *feels*, the intended intimacy of the exchange, one-on-one. His co-trainer, who knows him well, gives a shout of laughter and calls him a slut. Guillaume tells me this story later because he knows it will make me laugh, but I think about it for many years afterwards. Is speaking exclusively to each listener transgressive in its intimacy? Is it the same with writing? Is that what is seductive, as David Allison writes, in Nietzsche's address? Is that why Irigaray calls her treatment of Nietzsche intimate, erotic? *Écriture séduisante.* Is that all seduction is, in the end? How we address each other?

Poor old Nietzsche never had a chance at intimacy, never managed to have a single significant romantic relationship, despite desperately wanting one and making a terrible fool of himself on a number of occasions, proposing marriage to women he had just met. This element of his biography always makes me feel tenderly about him, despite the persistent sexism of his writing. I guess he got Irigaray in the end, as a romantic partner, if that counts for anything – and of course it doesn't.

French (Part III)

Lahiri writes of English and Italian as duelling siblings (Romulus and Remus? I wonder) with Italian as the newborn and English as the recalcitrant older teenage brother. I find this metaphor uncomfortable, mostly because I dislike the idea of mothering anything other than my two children. As I read this I wonder if that is partly why I am obnoxious about improving my French – because I refuse to coddle, coax, raise it lovingly? These days I chuck my French in the deep end and expect it to sink or swim – mostly I manage to keep my head above water, but without style: gulping, thrashing about. 'Désolée,' I say breezily to my mother-in-law on the phone. 'Mon français est vraiment dans la poubelle ce soir.' *Sorry – my French is really in the bin tonight.*

And yet, at some point, I realise that I have to stop reading translations, I have to stop reading subtitles, because my brain is working overtime trying to assess the quality of the translation and tracking and grabbing at new vocabulary, and all of the pleasure of reading books and watching films and television is subordinated to my critical, nit-picking brain.

I never meant to get to this point – I did not want to have to get by on what is mine alone, in terms of French, in the bank. In French I am poor. But imagine if you were poor and also constantly calculating the exchange rate of every word against a global index that was designed to cheat you out of real understanding? Keeping you distant from the real meaning? I grow cynical and turn the subtitles off, sit down reluctantly with the original, to give that part of my brain a break. And here's where something absurd happens: *it's not hard.* I understand almost all of it. I am shocked. When did I learn how to drive?

*

Okay, so understanding is not the same as *understanding*. But either I cannot be as poor in French as I think I am, or the cost of superficial comprehension is cheaper than I thought. Have I racked up more in the bank over a decade of raising bilingual children with a Frenchman than I thought? Or is it just not that hard, once you commit to letting go?

Blissful Isles

There is no place to which I return, in my thoughts and in my writings, as often as I return to Shiraishi Island. Shiraishi is a tiny island off the coast of Japan's main island of Honshū. It is part of a chain of thirty-one islands that make up the Kasaoka Islands in the Seto Inland Sea, of which only seven are inhabited. Shiraishi Island is covered in forest and dense with life: beetles, crabs, birds, fish, and lizards. In August the sea sparkles like handfuls of noisy diamonds. A villa for international visitors is perched on the side of a hill with a wooden balcony that overlooks the bay. A narrow walking track runs downhill from the entrance of the villa to the sandy cove, and it takes about ten minutes, with young children, to reach the water's edge.

I stayed on Shiraishi Island at a time when my children were very young. It was our first summer in Japan. We had moved to Kansai Gaidai University in Osaka prefecture with the restless energy of perpetual travellers, and I had accepted a full-time teaching contract that came with accommodation on campus even though we did not speak the language, did not know the culture.

One evening at a restaurant my daughter asked shyly for some ice for her apple juice and I looked at her blankly, realising that I had brought my children to eat at a restaurant without any way of

161

communicating with the staff. I had neither a working phone nor a dictionary. 'No,' I had replied in shock as I understood the enormity of what we had done. 'No, I cannot ask for ice, I do not know how.' Shaking my head. 'We must drink the juice warm.'

The move to Japan was thrilling and disorientating in ways that felt familiar, seductive and exhausting. I was the most seduced; I was the most exhausted. My husband worked on his research and the children attended a local kindergarten in crisp green and white uniforms with clip-on bowties. I spent hours failing to google the right combination of words that would lead me to a blog post that might explain how to help them settle into a school in which neither they, nor we, spoke the language.

Each morning I dragged myself to class, stacking cans of black coffee from the vending machine on top of armfuls of worksheets. Workdays were filled with lecturing and tutoring and marking and gazing out the window of my classroom at the traffic while my students completed assignments. I began to see shadowy creatures out of the corner of my eye during the day, and at night they gathered in our apartment and sat with heads bowed, faces hidden by conical hats, blocking my path to the window, to the sink for a glass of water, forcing me back into bed to stare sleeplessly at the shoji panels from my futon on the tatami floor.

While this shift in our lives felt seismic, it was nothing compared to the earthquake that hit soon after we arrived. The epicentre was five kilometres from the university and the quake was major, causing structural damage and tripping long-dormant fault lines. The children were delighted at first, laughing at my husband, who had ushered them outside in his pyjamas once the tremor had subsided. But as the summer wore on and the humidity increased, the earth continued to convulse and spasm in fits of aftershock. We were told that there was a serious risk of more deadly tremors to come. Everyone was anxious. The children begged us to let them sleep in helmets. Scaffolding was erected around our apartment block in order to check for cracks and fractures in the brick. The scaffolding was shrouded in a fabric to protect workers from the sun, enclosing us day and night inside a dark cocoon.

The aftershocks ranged from frightening to confusing. Sometimes when I was walking I felt my knees buckle; I could not tell if it was me wobbling, or the earth. I'd always trusted the ground as something solid and secure, but that spring I learned the earth could be just as unstable as I was. The children were sent home from their kindergarten with cushions we had to label with their names and addresses. A friend explained that although they looked like cushions they doubled as protection in case of another major earthquake – the children were taught to slip them on their heads as they hid under tables. The labelling was to help rescue teams identify bodies in case they were buried in rubble.

The days passed, and the earth and I continued, disturbed and disturbing, trying to settle into something that resembled stability, whilst heaving and flexing with an unpredictability that troubled me. One day I walked the entire length of the university corridors, twice, looking for an earring I believed lost but which in reality I had never even owned. I waited for classes to end and summer break to begin, but new pressures emerged. The humidity mounted and the scream of cicadas never seemed to abate. The little creatures in conical hats goaded me; I left the house early each morning to write poetry before the children woke, but instead I sat sweating at my desk in the dark, hounded by the screech of cicadas, filling page after page with images of flint axes being sharpened, of tin-monkeys in a woodchipper, of scratched records being smashed against a brick wall.

When a group of friends casually invited us to Shiraishi Island to escape the monotony of summer heat I was so grateful I had to hold back tears; I was in such a state of desperation I was ready to run there barefoot.

*

The day we arrived there was a typhoon warning, and as a precaution the ferry to Shiraishi Island had been closed. It was late August. The heat had become outrageous – a sticky, sweaty heat that unpicked the laws of time and space and made everything seem eternal, buoyant. Travelling with us were a couple of hooligans who lived above us and had a daughter the same age as ours. I had mentally given the couple this nickname, *the hooligans*, clocking that they both had a wayward relationship with rules. I was hyperalert to this because I was desperately trying to establish a sense of the rules and norms in order not to transgress them, not to offend or seem ungrateful. It was an affectionate nickname; I liked the way her eyes lit up with a sneaky magic when she told me about refusing to conform to the social expectations she had been raised with, the way she slowed down when she cussed in English in order to enunciate correctly. I liked the way he ignored traffic signals, was dismissive of authority. I had once, from the window of my classroom, seen him veering widely around a traffic guard to cross the street illegally, his daughter perched on the back of his bicycle, both waving merrily to the guard shouting at them.

After wandering around the dock, stopping to chat to fishermen and point at the choppy sea, the hooligans returned to tell us they'd bribed a middle-aged man in a red bandana to take us on his speedboat out to the island over the surging waves. Someone asked about lifejackets for the children and the man in the bandana gestured dismissively towards the hull. I sat under the hard top, hugging my son on my lap. The men gripped on at the back as water crashed against them, soaking them to the skin. The children shrieked with laughter, sticky with lemonade ice blocks, full of glee at the unexpectedly rough crossing.

The typhoon raged overnight but we woke in our rental villa to the same lush air, a few broken branches, and a soaked deck. Any memory of the storm had evaporated by mid-morning when we all

164

tumbled down the mountainside and collapsed into the clear water. 'I wanna take the girls out to that island,' one of the hooligans said, pointing at a reef a half kilometre in the distance. In the haze of heat I could make out a red torii gate perched on a rocky outcrop. I nodded, uneasy, and we swam out through the sparkling waters with one-armed strokes, dragging our daughters, who lounged and splashed in inflatable swim rings. Near the shrine, the girls found a coral-coloured crustacean that they took turns cupping in their palms. They asked us what it was called, but neither of us knew.

The holiday passed in a laze of half-read books and children messing around with old guitars with broken strings, scrambling up and down the mountain from the villa to the sea. My son began to speak to everyone in a jumble of French, English, and Japanese. My daughter and her friend discovered a fig tree at the top of the hill and took to sneaking out of the villa at dawn to feast on wild figs for breakfast.

On one of the last nights, the-swim-out-to-the-island-hooligan was hauling his daughter and mine from the ocean and hurling them, shrieking, through the air to splash back into the darkening sea as the sun set in a blaze of ruby and gold. I took photos of them from the shoreline, shadows tumbling through the air in explosions of limbs and laughter. I had a sudden memory of being tossed into a river by my favourite uncle, the one who often came to play with us kids when he had grown bored of the adults. I remembered that I had come, once, from a family of hooligans. I remembered a life before the fatigue, before the earthquake. I remembered what it felt like to not be afraid.

We stayed on Shiraishi Island for a week, returning on the ferry, which had resumed operations once the typhoon had passed. After four seasons in Japan and two more typhoons we returned to

Australia, trading in a flurry of snowflakes and eggnog for heatwaves and bushfires. Our life in Japan soon began to feel like an aberration, an intermission, a hiatus from real life. 'Japan was a nice experiment,' I wrote to a friend upon our return, 'but there is only so long you can live inside an experiment.' Shiraishi Island became an idyll within a memory of an experiment; a dream within a dream.

As the years pass, I find that, rather than fading, my memories and daydreams of the place seem to be growing, like lichen. In my writing I call it 'the island' and watch it derail my attempts to follow other paths, to write other stories: a red thread of nostalgia that I keep following back to the heart of a labyrinth I cannot escape; Ariadne in love with the island of Naxos.

The other path I'm meant to be following is the philosophy of Nietzsche – his writings on nihilism and revaluation are the foundation of a project I began many years ago, a project that seems to have no end. I soon discover Nietzsche was also obsessed with an island. His, too, was far from his homeland, and his, too, offered a sun-soaked respite from the pressures of work and diminishing health. Nietzsche's was the volcanic Ischia, off the coast of Naples, a place he discovered whilst staying in Sorrento in 1876–77. Nietzsche was thirty-two and suffering from a variety of maladies including crippling migraines. Exhausted with his professorship in Basel, he had been invited to recuperate in Sorrento by his friend Malwida von Meysenbug, and they stayed in the Villa Rubinacci with other young writers and students.

Nietzsche spent his days convalescing, enjoying the climate and company, engaging in long philosophical and literary discussions with the other guests. For the first time in many years, Nietzsche had the luxury of being able to reflect uninterrupted, and he filled notebooks and letters with ideas and aphorisms that would go on to become some of his most famous works, including *Human, All Too Human* and *Thus Spoke Zarathustra*. Although Nietzsche's health did not dramatically improve, it was a crucial time for him intellectually, an idyllic and formative period of his life.

Nietzsche could see Ischia from the terrace of his room in Sorrento – in fact, he could see both the island and the peak of Vesuvius, almost as mirror images of each other in the bay. It was here that Nietzsche experienced the first tremors of the rupture that would end his passionate friendship with Richard Wagner, and this break, along with his time at the Villa Rubinacci, marked a major turning point in his life and work. In a passionate study of Nietzsche's writings from this period, Paolo D'Iorio explains that it was in Sorrento that Nietzsche turned away from a future in academia and accepted his destiny as a 'wandering philosopher'.

The island of Ischia looms large in Nietzsche's *Thus Spoke Zarathustra*. Some scholars claims Ischia was the inspiration for the *glückseligen Inseln*, Zarathustra's 'blessed' or 'blissful' islands, which represent a joyful refuge for the wandering prophet, far from the isolation of Zarathustra's mountain dwelling and the unsympathetic masses in the towns and cities. At the beginning of Part II, Zarathustra wakes before dawn, overcome by the urge to travel to the islands in order to share his philosophy with friends and disciples. 'I have belonged to solitude too long,' Zarathustra realises. 'I have become nothing but speech and the tumbling of a brook from high rocks: I want to hurl my words down into the valleys . . . I want to sail across broad seas like a cry and a shout of joy, until I find the Blissful Islands where my friends are waiting . . .'

The Blissful Islands have been described as a sort of Epicurean garden, a place of intellectual freedom and companionship, untainted by the demands and pressures of everyday life. Peter Groff observes that 'the Blessed Isle of Ischia had represented for Nietzsche his original liberation from what Epicurus had once called "the prison of daily duties and politics", the vision of a sequestered friendship community of like-minded free spirits'. On the Blissful Islands, Zarathustra and his teachings are valued. The prophet announces his arrival by comparing himself to the North Wind, arriving to shake ripe figs from the trees to fall into the hands of his disciples so that they can enjoy the sweet flesh and juices of his teachings. A significant portion of Part II of the book passes here on the islands, with Zarathustra developing his teachings in dialogue with an engaged and attentive audience.

It is a shock, therefore, when Zarathustra realises that he cannot stay in this idyll (one cannot live inside a dream). He realises the threat of intellectual stagnation in this friendly utopia, and Zarathustra understands that he will never fulfill his potential if he does not force himself back into the difficult and generative solitude of his mountain dwelling. It is a bitter decision for the lonely prophet, who has embraced the companionship of these days on the islands. He tears himself away in sorrow to make the overnight journey to the coast on foot, to sail with the boat at dawn.

Zarathustra never returns to the Blissful Islands, but they haunt the rest of the work and re-emerge at two crucial moments later in the text: first, when the Soothsayer, the nihilist prophet, claims that the Blissful Islands no longer exist; and again, at the end, when Zarathustra declares that his friends and disciples are coming – that his beloved companions have travelled from the Blissful Islands to be with him in his mountain dwelling.

In 1883, Nietzsche planned to spend the summer on the island of Ischia with his sister but changed his mind and went to Sils-Maria in Switzerland instead. At the height of that summer, an earthquake devastated Ischia, killing thousands of people. The tragedy upset Nietzsche terribly and soon after the earthquake, he wrote to a friend:

The fate of Ischia shocks me more and more; and aside from what concerns everyone else, there is something about it that touches me personally, in a haunting way that is entirely my own.

Nietzsche's extensive notes, written after the earthquake in preparation for the third and fourth parts of Zarathustra, indicate that the sinking of the Blissful Islands, and the impossibility of returning to them, was to be a major narrative crisis and a reckoning for Zarathustra, an irreversible loss that would force the prophet to face his destiny. Instead, in the final version, this idea is reduced to the Soothsayer's discouraging comment that they simply 'no longer exist'. This pronouncement disturbs Zarathustra, who goes on to deny it – almost maniacally – saying, 'No! No! Thrice no!' Zarathustra mutters, seemingly to himself, that there are still blissful islands, declaring that the gloomy prophet knows nothing of these things.

Ischia may have been destroyed by an earthquake, but Ischia was only a place, after all; an Epicurean garden could, with care, be established elsewhere. In theory, the spirit of the place could be cultivated by a gathering of like-minded companions in any location. At the end of *Thus Spoke Zarathustra*, this seems possible, as the lonely prophet claims to hear his beloved companions drawing near. Perhaps Zarathustra, who has finally unburdened himself of his most difficult idea, that of *eternal recurrence*, will now permit himself to relax in an Epicurean utopia. The question of whether the Blissful Islands still exist is abandoned.

As Nietzsche confessed in his letter to Peter Gast, earthquakes can feel eerily symbolic when they shake and shatter locations of personal significance. Nietzsche avoided the earthquake in Ischia, but not the one in Nice in the early months of 1887 that destroyed his room in the Pension de Genève, where he had composed the third and fourth parts of *Thus Spoke Zarathustra*.

In contrast, although the epicentre of my earthquake was only five kilometres from where we lived, it did not disturb or devastate a place that held meaning for me, and there were very few casualties compared to the Ischian earthquake of 1883. The Japanese earthquake did not stop me from travelling to Shiraishi Island – rather, the earthquake and subsequent aftershocks were propelling forces, part of the maddening cocktail that made the early days of that summer unendurable. What sank our island and made it impossible to return to was the pandemic. Australian borders snapped shut and we were reminded, forcefully, of the precise parameters of our own enormous island-continent.

Nietzsche had originally planned that the sinking of the islands would function as a reckoning for Zarathustra, and one that would propel him towards his destiny and Nietzsche's greatest contribution to philosophy. I long to believe that such a thing is possible. That we can turn, however brutally, however violently, personal tragedy and catastrophe into part of the necessary journey of realising the meaning and purpose of our lives. I do not know if it is true, but this is part of the appeal of Nietzsche: the promise of gleaning value from our grief and failures.

Because I am haunted by an island and because I am struggling with meaning, I try, as I read, to place myself within Zarathustra in order to locate a path forward. It is difficult. I am conflicted. The tension between the locales and their classical associations is too much, even for Zarathustra, who never settles anywhere. The harsh polis (Plato?); the blissful isles (Epicurus?); the mountain dwelling (Dionysus?). I find myself drawn to Zarathustra's transit between places, the liminal, marginal moments. I feel affinity with the prophet during his agonising overnight trek to the boat that will lead away from his friends, away from the joy and community of the Blissful Isles. I can't help feeling that these moments of transit do not belong to any philosopher, but rather to the poets, to Homer, perhaps. What is *The Odyssey*, after all, but an epic journey between states of being, between isles?

Once on the boat, Zarathustra struggles with his grief for many days and nights. Nietzsche writes that he was 'cold and deaf for sorrow', with 'riddles and bitterness in his heart'. I still grieve what has been – what has *had to be* – given up. But I maintain a stubborn faith that I will turn, at some point, and say, 'I am again alone and willingly so, alone with the pure sky and the open sea . . .' as Zarathustra does, once he is four days' journey from the Blissful Isles. And that all of this sinking and quaking and grieving will reverberate and produce something of value.

My Naxos, my Ischia, continues to haunt me in a 'way that is entirely my own'. I write Shiraishi Island again and again. I write of reading Yasunari Kawabata's *Snow Country* on the balcony. I write of the moment I stood on that tiny island next to a vermillion torii gate, holding a crustacean in my hands and seeing the light twinkle loudly on the water of the bay. I write of the dreams I had when I was there, full of wild figs and flying fish and reckless glee. I write of the fecundity of the island, the lush green, the tropical air. I write of the children's sticky shouts, their lazy, animal-like sprawling on the balcony. I write of the heavy kayaks lying on the wet sand. I write about the tender white strips of squid blackened with charcoal that we ate on the beach as the sun began to sink. I write about chasing a hat that had been whipped off a small head and was careering down the beach, feeling faster than I had ever felt before, every muscle a piston, my legs impossibly long, outrunning the wind. I write about climbing the mountain back up to the villa and my little son, four years old, putting his hand in mine and puffing, 'This *yama* is so *okii*.'

But most often I write of the fish that leapt out of the water, the fish you could see from the balcony of the villa, looking down at the bay. Their sharp, wild little bodies shooting dramatically out of the water, self-propelled by their own muscular biology, gliding through the hot air, cheating death.

Nietzsche is not the only writer haunted by Ischia. Ischia is also the island of escape and reckoning for Lenù, the heroine of Elena Ferrante's Neapolitan quartet. Ischia is Lenù's first taste of life outside of the impoverished neighbourhood in which she has grown up, away from the tense alliances and violent antagonisms of her childhood. Lenù travels to the island during the summer of her fifteenth year, sent by her teacher, Maestra Oliviero, to recover after a difficult year of study. Lenù's mother is annoyed by the Maestra's interference in their lives, saying spitefully, 'The signorina must go and rest on Ischia, the signorina is too exhausted. Go and make dinner, go on, or I'll hit you.' During the journey to the ferry to Ischia, Lenù's mother is increasingly distressed by the thought of her daughter's solitary trip across the ocean, terrified that the crossing will be rough. She berates her daughter for not remembering their summers in Coroglio when she was a child, for not remembering learning to swim.

The crossing is not rough, Lenù does not drown, and on Ischia life is pleasant – Lenù helps with the housework but is otherwise free to enjoy the sun, the beach, and to read. In her own words, she blossoms. But the idyll does not last: Donato Sarratore, the father of her beloved Nino, ambushes Lenù in her bed on the night of her fifteenth birthday. Aroused, repulsed, and horrified, Lenù rises before dawn the next morning to flee at first light, hurrying to the ferry with her hastily packed things.

Lenù returns to the island a few summers later to experience even more shocking and humiliating reckonings, one of which becomes the impetus for her first novel, which she writes many years later in a sudden and violent attempt at catharsis. Lenù writes the novel in a frenzy, over a period of twenty days, in her apartment at the University of Pisa. She does nothing else as she writes, completely ignoring her fiancé and her doctoral thesis. Flicking back through the finished work, she is not particularly impressed, but a sense of calm returns, and she feels able to move on. She gives the handwritten manuscript to her fiancé as a gift that she calls 'foolish, but . . . truly mine'. Her fiancé's mother, an editor, instantly recognises the potential of the work. The book is published, and Lenù's life as a writer begins.

In literature, islands are often sites of trickery and transformation, places in which destinies are simultaneously thwarted, rerouted, and forged. In Shakespeare's *The Tempest*, Prospero's island is a place of sorcery, and Prospero manipulates the other characters with the magic he has mastered whilst living in exile. Islands are set apart, and what they offer is abstraction – elsewhere, other, beyond. Depending on the narrative – depending on the character – this can be a source of respite or terror, or both. As in *The Odyssey*, islands can easily function as both paradise and prison. Islands operate as places where destinies are shaped, where gods and sorcerers live and toy with our fates. They also function as catalysts for what already exists within us, hothouses for our most potent desires.

But if we are passing through, if we are not confined to an island, then isn't what matters what we *bring back* with us? What Zarathustra goes on to achieve once he has left the Blissful Islands? What Lenù does with the shame of her teenage experiences on Ischia? What Nietzsche forged out of the pain of the devastation of Ischia? In D'Iorio's analysis, for Nietzsche, 'Ischia does not represent nostalgia and the memory of the past, but the place where volcanic subterranean forces penetrate the sea of forgetting to return into the light of the sun'. Islands, I begin to think, can shape destinies, but those destinies can only take shape once you are able to leave them behind – once you move on.

*

173

I write Shiraishi again and again. Sometimes I feel that I will never stop writing Shiraishi.

> Sorry, we could not calculate walking directions from 'Adelaide, SA 5000' to 'Shiraishi Island, Shiraishijima, Kasaoka, Okayama 714–0036, Japan'

> – Google Maps, November 2021

An excerpt from my notebook, titled *Island Fragments*:

Once, on a lush Japanese island in the wake of a typhoon I sat on the deck of a villa, looking down the rolling mountainside at a bay. Children were calling to each other and fish were leaping out of the glittering waters in wide arcs. On the beach, locals were grilling squid over hot charcoal. I sat in the wide heat with Kawabata's pitiless *Snow Country* open in my lap, not reading, just watching, lazily playing at naming all the variations of green I could see – chartreuse, lime, forest, emerald, pine. Earlier that day I had hiked up the mountain with my son, who had paused to sigh, 'This *yama* is so *okii*,' his small legs tired out by the steep path.

If that fish leaps again, I suddenly thought, noticing a particularly frenetic vault out of the water, *I will never be this happy again*. And the fish leapt again, thrice, four times, as if to say *Never! Never! Never!*

The Feeling
of Living

Art is neither the total rejection, nor the total acceptance, of all that is. It is a simultaneous rejection and acceptance, and that is why it can only be a perpetually renewed tearing apart. The artist exists invariably in this ambiguity, incapable of denying the real, and yet eternally bound to contest its eternal incompleteness.

– Albert Camus, 'Discours de Suède' ('Nobel Prize Speeches')

READING CAMUS

I begin to read in French. I am, again, shocked by how easy it is. Somewhere or sometime in between my husband babbling away to our babies in French and being surrounded by French pop music and chatting to Solange and translating for my in-laws and listening to my children make bilingual jokes I have . . . learned French? I start with Camus because, well, everyone starts with Camus, but also because he was a gorgeous French-Algerian loner who was interested in Nietzsche, and all of those things appeal to me, too.

THE SUN

One of the confusing things about my books is that, unlike my clothes, I have very little sense of where they have come from. In my copy of Camus' *L'Étranger*, the previous owner has scrawled notes on every page, some in English, some in French, marking passages of the text that are about the sun with a little sketch of a sun in the margins. There are a lot of little suns in the margins.

EXPERIMENT

Camus was an experiment. Would French, could French, lead me elsewhere, as Italian had led Lahiri? Could I find within myself some other self, some other plane? Could I, via French, find an internal *ailleurs*? Could I cultivate some rich, uncomfortable, even unnatural quest inwards? Would French, could French, be a language in which I might lose myself, one that could be creatively dangerous for me? Would the abyss be fertile?

TRANSLATION

I remember hearing the great Spanish poet Rafael Alberti read . . . Alberti read his poems in Spanish and his American translator, Ben Belitt, read them in English. Ben was sober, shy, outwardly conservative; he wore a tweed jacket and tie. Alberti gave Ben a toy pistol, what was called a cap gun, a toy capable of making very loud noises, and told Ben to shoot himself in the head whenever he, Alberti, gave the signal, and that is exactly what happened: Alberti would be reading in Spanish, pause, look at Ben, and Ben would reluctantly shoot himself in the head. But when Ben read the poems in English, Alberti had the pistol and from time to time shot himself in the head with real gusto. I felt it was a great lesson in translation.

– Mary Ruefle, 'I remember, I remember'

HIKING

I develop a malady I jokingly call 'Nietzsche Neck'. My neck and shoulders are cramped and painful; I wake with bad headaches and can't sit at my computer or read for long periods. The only things that seem to help are long, solitary walks in the bush near my house. I decide that my project is no longer about writing but about hiking. How it is going depends on how many hours I have spent tramping through the bush.

In John Kaag's *Hiking with Nietzsche*, Kaag hikes the trails above the Swiss town of Sils Maria where Nietzsche composed most of *Thus Spoke Zarathustra*. Kaag explains:

Walking is practically and physically beneficial, but it has also, for artists and thinkers like Nietzsche, been intimately tied to creation and philosophical thought . . . The history of philosophy is largely the history of thought in transit . . . The Buddha, Socrates, Aristotle, the Stoics, Jesus, Kant, Rousseau, Thoreau – these thinkers were never still for very long.

Where else can walking lead, I wonder – what other elsewheres might you access? Kaag also cautions that 'once you begin to hike, it is extremely hard to ever fully come to rest'. This is also part of the drama: I refuse to fully come to rest.

BLOOD

One morning I find myself at a university symposium about blood, unsure of why, listlessly trying to convince myself that investigating the link between blood and poetic insight will be of value to my thinking about Nietzsche, nihilism, and creativity. There are very few people; my head aches, I cannot find my pen. The first talk I have signed up for is about perceptions of blood in ancient Greek medicine. The speaker explains what is called *haematocentric* reasoning – the location of human intellect and rational thought *in the blood*. The Hippocratic corpus, for example, includes this line: 'The intelligence of man . . . is nourished not from the gut by food and drinks, but by a pure and luminous bath coming from a distillate of the blood.' A young scholar then introduces the Empedoclean belief that blood is the most superior substance, a perfect balance of the four primal elements of fire, water, air, and earth. Empedocles argued that blood was the seat not just of our intellect, but also our reason and understanding:

> [the heart is] nourished in seas of blood which leaps back and forth,
> and there especially it is called understanding by men;
> for men's understanding is blood around the heart

Empedocles' views on blood are not widely shared. The ancient Greek philosopher Theophrastus thought the idea of blood as the seat of reason and understanding was 'totally absurd'. I like Empedocles' ideas, though. Knowing might not happen in the blood, but the blood *knows* things. The speaker at the lectern makes a quick aside about the diagnostic importance of dreams in ancient Greek medical texts. 'If you dream of a dry river,' she says, 'it means your blood is sick, and you have got to get that sorted.' 'How?' a woman in the front row asks, leaning forward suddenly. The answer is vague – rather than cures, the ancient texts focus on interpreting and diagnosing what the blood says. I peer carefully at the woman in the front row, trying to figure out if her blood has been speaking to her, too.

Écriture Séduisante

There's something easy and seductive about Camus. Women worshipped him – I would have, too, I'm weak like that, easily undone by a strong jaw and thick, swept-back hair. There is something lonely about Camus, too, and I've always been attracted to lonely men – deeply lonely men, who live with the knowledge they'll never find solace: there's a thrill in loving men like that, the thrill of profound distance, and freedom.

Blood (Part II)

I was once given a clear, viscous soup at a class picnic, variously translated as being made of 'bitter fungus' and 'ear mushrooms'. My students presented it to me in a red Tupperware container, explaining it was traditional Chinese medicine 'for my blood'. They seemed shy about giving it to me. I did not understand that the soup was a response to what my blood was telling them; they were embarrassed because they knew I was sick, and they knew I did not know. 'My students made me soup for my blood,' I said gleefully to my husband later, presuming it was just another of the tender, eccentric gifts I had become used to receiving, like the cushions with my children's faces printed on them.

Years after the blood soup I was diagnosed, of course, with catastrophically low iron levels. My blood *was* sick. My doctor smoothed out the results on her desk and said, 'Honestly, I'm surprised you made it to this appointment. I've never seen levels so low.' I felt the scaffolding I had erected around my fatigue collapse. 'I thought it was depression,' I said slowly. 'I'm still going running.' I had not dreamed of dry rivers, but my blood had been clamouring about the deficit, the rage of lack roaring in my ears and chest. I had been waking at night to sob with an inarticulate grief. I had dismissed it as jetlag, heartache, anxiety. My blood had been screaming at me for iron and I had tried to treat it with exercise and mindfulness. 'Oh no,' my doctor said briskly. 'You can't run your way out of this. We need to intervene.'

This all happened a few years after my children were born. As I was making their lives, in pregnancy, in childbirth, while breastfeeding, I had the feeling that I was dying. That life was leaking out of me and into them. I did not resent it – I wanted my babies to thrive – but for years I felt like a ghoulish shadow-self, undernourished and pale. Becoming the haggard portrait in the attic seemed a reasonable trade-off for the plump, laughing babies I had made. Each morning I caught the bus to work past a billboard advertising black coffee and a steak sandwich. WAKE UP AND STEAK UP! the ad shouted. There was noise in my body whenever I saw it. A bristle of electricity, a magnetic pull. I'd even find myself thinking *wakeupandsteakup* throughout the day, like an uncontrollable mantra. It seems so pitiful, in retrospect – my blood trying to communicate with me by learning to speak my language like a desperate foreigner, shouting the slogan of a fast-food restaurant at me. And me, refusing to believe that the body had any language other than pain.

After my diagnosis I had two iron infusions that dripped their cold, rust-coloured medicine into my veins, gave me a migraine, and made me feel so robust I wept with relief.

THE PLAGUE

I have read *La Peste* twice already, both times in English. The first time I was in my early twenties and minding a makeshift bookstore in a garage on a country lane in Suffolk. I was paid in books, and sometimes when the pub across the lane was busy, I took a break to work there, where I was paid in pints. The days were sunny but it was damp in the garage, and I warmed myself with a small electric heater and a thermos of hot black coffee. I struggled through *The Plague*, wanting to like it more than I did, finding it bleak and unsympathetic. I couldn't get a foothold on the plot, was bored by the philosophical digressions, didn't care for any of the characters or their obscure pandemic. I persisted because I had found it useful, sometimes, to persist with novels I did not like, but it did not satisfy me even after I finished. I agreed with the French critics and philosophers who dismissed it as 'grey and heavy' and 'the dullest of Camus's books'.

Many years later when our own pandemic began, I reread it, and found myself again alienated, scowling now and again about the fame of the novel as a work of allegorical genius with its silent and absent women, and not a single reference to the domestic insecurity and violence that increase in times of crisis. It's a notable omission because the novel is all about violence – there's the unpredictable, inexplicable violence of the plague itself; the violence of isolation, enforced by the military; Tarrou's meditation on the violence inherent in the democratic state; there is even the violence of Christian morality, with Father Paneloux raging at his followers to embrace the horror of the plague as God's will. But the violence of the home is not addressed at all.

I have rarely been bothered by a lack of female characters in literature, and I was surprised at how annoyed I felt by their absence in *The Plague*. It probably had something to do with watching my mum lose her job as a travel agent, and thinking about how much worse the pandemic was for her, a woman over sixty in casual employment. And reflecting again on how much worse it would have been if the pandemic had struck a decade earlier when her situation had been even more precarious.

When she told me she had been retrenched I asked her what she would do. 'Probably just drink and smoke,' she quipped, with the sardonic tenacity I've always admired.

FREEDOM

. . . all the older forms of literature were hardened and set by the time she became a writer. The novel alone was young enough to be soft in her hands – another reason, perhaps, why she wrote novels. Yet . . . who shall say that even this most pliable of all forms is rightly shaped for her use? No doubt we shall find her knocking that into shape for herself when she has the free use of her limbs; and providing some new vehicle, not necessarily in verse, for the poetry in her. For it is the poetry that is still denied outlet.

– Virginia Woolf, *A Room of One's Own*

ÉCRITURE SÉDUISANTE (PART II)

These days I seem to spend a lot of the time I am meant to be writing watching interviews with the American comedian Awkwafina. I have a crush on her because I'm weak like that, easily seduced by a sharp jawline and hawk eyes and swept-up black hair. She's got that sharp solitude that I love, too, edgy and uncomfortable, like Camus. I tool around on the internet like everyone else, laughing at memes about lockdown. I buy clothes online; I wear eyeliner. Who knows who and how to be, in times like these?

TREES

When my daughter was not yet two, she began to gleefully shout out the words for the objects she could see – house, car, tree, dog. One morning I was driving her to day care, when she piped up from the back seat, 'Maman? Maman?' And I said, 'Yes?' and she said, 'Maman, maman, TREE, Maman, TREE. . . Papa, Papa, ARBRE. Papa, ARBRE'. I said, 'Yes, Maman says TREE and Papa says ARBRE, that's right, Maman speaks English and Papa speaks French.' And my daughter said, 'Maman TREE Papa ARBRE, et . . . Et moi? Moi?' I looked in the rear-view mirror and saw her face alert and confused. 'Oh!' I said joyfully, realising her conundrum. 'Well, you say whatever you want! You have both languages, French and English. But probably you will use TREE when speaking to Maman and ARBRE when speaking to Papa.' She nodded, content with this answer, and then pointed to a large eucalyptus, shouting at the top of her lungs, 'TREE!'

MUMMIFY

'A mummification' is how one scholar describes Luce Irigaray's treatment of Nietzsche, and I immediately think of my own project. Is that what mothers do, do we shroud, do we *mummify?* Am I, in this work, attempting a mummification of Nietzsche? A *maman*ification?

BLOOD (PART III)

Another talk at the symposium about blood is an analysis of the blood sacrifice that revives the dead in Homer's *The Odyssey*. Odysseus travels to the underworld to consult the blind Theban prophet, Tiresias.

To communicate with the dead, Odysseus must perform a complex ritual that ends with the slaughter of two sheep, slitting their throats to bleed their rich dark blood into a pit. *Wakeupandsteakup!* I think. Odysseus stands guard as the souls swarm towards the sacrificial blood, holding them at bay for Tiresias to drink first. Odysseus is so intent on his task he won't even let his mother Anticlea near the blood until Tiresias has drunk. But Odysseus does not forget her. Once he has his prophecy, he begs one last piece of information from the seer. 'Tell me this,' he implores Tiresias. 'I see the spirit of my dead mother. She sits in silence by the blood and cannot bring herself to look her own son in the face or say a single word to him. Tell me, my lord, how can I make her recognize who I am?' 'Any ghost to whom you give access to the blood will speak the truth,' Tiresias answers. 'Any to whom you deny it will withdraw.'

Access blood, access truth. In Latin, the word for blood is *sanguis*. Many English words have evolved from this root. Sanguine means optimistic, or hopeful. Sangfroid, that cold-bloodedness, means self-possession, especially in the face of strain. Consanguineous means 'descended from the same ancestor'. Blood can reveal more than illness and ignorance. It can also hold answers to haunting family histories, categorical proof of origin, and stories in place of the absence and loss that can define a life.

FREEDOM (PART II)

You can guess how fundamentally melancholy and despondent I am . . . All I ask is some freedom . . . I become outraged at the many, uncountably many, unfreedoms that imprison me.

– Nietzsche, letter to von Gersdorff

184

More Interruptions

One morning when we wake there are four espresso cups in the kitchen that my daughter has filled with terrorising notes. Two of the notes say 'Merry Christmas', and the other two say: 'You're gonna die'.

Mummify (Part II)

Besides my failure to return to Paris, another failed aspect of my research is that I had initially thought I would investigate the lack of women in nihilism studies, as well as the lack of scholars and writers whose work was considered, like that of Camus and Beckett, to be deeply engaged with questions of nihilism and meaning. I wanted to explore Cynthia Enloe's iconic question, *Where are the women?* I was deeply influenced by Irigaray's poetic accusations of Nietzsche and Zarathustra in *Marine Lover*, especially her anger at his denial of maternal origins. Kelly Oliver, author of *Womanizing Nietzsche: Philosophy's Relation to the Feminine*, explains that in Irigaray's critique of eternal recurrence she accuses Nietzsche of forgetting 'the maternal waters out of which all humans are born in favor of great heights, and the rarified air of mountaintops'.

Beckett does not forget these maternal waters. Beckett is drowning in them. Despite my irritation with *The Plague*, Camus also cannot be accused of forgetting his maternal waters – his unfinished book, *Le Premier Homme*, is a tender portrait of the two women who raised him, his mother and grandmother, and a celebration of his impoverished Algerian childhood.

Hannah Arendt also interrogates the theory of eternal recurrence in her work, as well as Nietzsche's writing on will, and willing. For Arendt, Nietzsche's weakness is his solitude, his insistence on the individual journey of becoming that does not value or account for community, responsibility, and belonging. I often think about his line regarding the preconditions for philosophy, that the philosopher must perhaps have been 'a critic and a skeptic and a dogmatist and historian and, moreover, a poet and collector and traveller and guesser of riddles and moralist and seer and "free spirit" and practically everything, in order to run through the range of human values and value feelings and *be able* to gaze with many eyes and consciences from the heights into every distance . . .' I think about it because the list so clearly does not include *all types*. Does not include some of the most profound identities we can assume: parent, child, sibling, carer, friend, lover, spouse.

But I'm trying to find a place where I can take off these identities, too. Trying to find a space for myself that does not commune, is not responsible, does not belong. Nietzsche isn't quite right for me but neither is Irigaray, nor is Arendt. I spend a lot of the summer reading Camus's essays at the beach, even when it is too hot, luxuriating in the sun, the salt, and the solitude (*le soleil, le sel, la solitude*). In 'Noces à Tipasa' ('Nuptials at Tipasa') I read:

> I love this life with abandon and wish to speak of it freely: it gives me pride in my human condition. I am often told that it's nothing to be proud of. But yes, it is : this sun, this sea, my heart leaping with youthfulness, my body tasting of salt, and the immense landscape before me in which tenderness and glory can be found in hues of yellow and blue.

I want to stay suspended in this state forever.

SOLITUDE

Contrary to popular opinion, if there is one who does not have the right to solitude, it is the artist. Art cannot be a monologue.

– Albert Camus, 'Discours de Suède' ('Nobel Prize Speeches')

MORE DREAMS

I had a dream, once, about a writer I know. In the dream I bumped into him and suddenly remembered a bone I had to pick with him. 'Why didn't you tell me?' I snapped at him. 'Why didn't you tell me how hard it is, to be a writer? How uncomfortable, how fucking *lonely*?' He laughed at me. 'Oh, that!' he said. 'There's an easy way to deal with it. The thing is . . .'

And then I woke up.

I told my husband about it the next morning. 'You should text him,' he said, with a mouthful of cereal. 'You should text and ask him. Hey, in the dream, what were you going to say? What's the thing?'

I thought about this for a while but then decided it was too weird, even for me. Also, I think I knew what the thing was. I had a feeling that in the dream he was going to say, 'The thing is *you just have to keep moving.*'

The writer comes to my house one day looking dreadful. He has stitches in his leg that require a longer convalescence than he had anticipated. 'I can't run – I can't dance!' he says in despair. I want to tell him of my dream, to insist that he has to keep moving – but instead I offer some platitudes about meditation. 'If this goes on for much longer, I will indeed have to resort to extreme measures,' he says darkly.

FLAUBERT

That nihilist! As I hike each morning I think of Nietzsche's riposte to Flaubert's expressed preference for sitting down to think: *Only ideas won by walking are of any value.*

> *Sit* as little as possible; give no credence to any thought that was not born outdoors while one moved about freely . . . The sedentary life – as I have said once before – is the real *sin* against the holy spirit.
>
> – Nietzsche, 'Why I Am So Clever'

ORIGINS

My family history is truncated at crucial points by a fierce refusal (by ancestors on both sides) to hold on to us, their progeny – children orphaned, disowned, given up for adoption. For a long time, I thought of it as a deficit, that I was lacking the necessary structure to truly know myself, or to give my children a sense of their own selves. My husband can trace his family back through the villages of Normandy for centuries. You are half French, I imagined telling my son and daughter, and half fabrication, half myth. Part Viking, part mystery. You are apples and smoke; you are boulevards and mist.

A few years ago I spat in a tube and received a map of my DNA. I could not fill in a family tree, but once the technology was available, I had access to my blood's ancestry. The results showed I was a mash-up of British and Scandinavian heritage. Most people were unimpressed. 'Have you never looked in a mirror?' friends asked. I had spent my life looking and wondering, but I could never decipher anything about my blue eyes, my freckled face, my dark blonde hair. It was a face that seemed to come from nowhere, be linked to nothing. My brother also spat into a tube and received a similar map of his DNA, but he was searching for answers to bigger questions than why we might pass as Norwegian. The database was sophisticated enough to identify us as siblings, and my brother kept a sharp eye on the DNA matches as the database expanded, looking for other possible relatives. Most were too distant to be of real interest until one Saturday morning when he found an unsettlingly significant match. *You and I have 3477cm over 57 segments and this guy and I have 1588cm over 75 segments*, he texted as I was cleaning the kids' bedroom. I stood staring at my phone, gripping a pirate puppet in the other hand. A second text came through almost immediately. *He also has the same surname as the man mum's birth mother married.* The man she married after putting up my mother for adoption the day she was born.

FRENCH, CONTINUED

I am not a Francophile. I do not love France, I do not love the sound of French, nor of myself speaking French. I still remember the physical discomfort of trying to produce French, the sense of panic, the way it made me flush. There was so much shame in it, so much impairment. I remember rushing up out of the métro one afternoon in Paris as part of a surging crowd of people, feeling pressed on all sides and myself on the heels of a lady who suddenly tripped and fell. She was older, frail, and the crowd split quickly as people stopped to offer help. I stopped, too, hoping to be useful, and she glared up at me and accused me of being responsible for her fall. I cannot remember what she said, exactly. I think I was only just able to grasp her fury, the gist of her accusation. Unable to respond or even to apologise, I gritted my teeth and shrugged, turning on my heel and striding

189

away. I later wondered what I would have said in English, struggling to imagine myself as the cause of an old lady's fall in any other city in the world.

BODIES

I think a lot about Miranda Kerr's body, mostly because of a short video I saw once on the *School of Life* website that offers Kerr's interest in yoga and eastern philosophy as evidence of the way that the west 'mishandles' its culture. Kerr finds answers in the east that she could easily find in the west, the speaker suggests, if only the west were better at disseminating those answers:

> She might have looked elsewhere. She might have found that Plato or Tolstoy had things to teach her. Maybe she could have been touched by Bach or medieval architecture. It's not as if the West doesn't also have a deep and long engagement with the sorrows of life. But, like so many spiritually curious people, she didn't end up engaging with its culture. Instead she joined the Soka Gakkai Buddhist movement.

Apart from being patronising garbage, I struggle with the entire premise of the piece. Kerr's interest in eastern traditions is clearly related to the way they are embedded in the body, in movement, meditation and breath. It is not just about addressing the sorrows or nihilism of life, but about rootedness, in the earth, the physical world – an investigation into existence as breath and muscle, the practice of being in the body. An attempt at inhabiting both the earthly and somatic experience of life, as well as the metaphysical questions that plague us all.

Reading Otherwise

Reading in French is slow. Slow like being underwater. Slow like learning to breathe through gills rather than with my lungs, like learning to shift breathing to another organ. Sometimes I have to forcibly submerge myself, denying myself the use of a dictionary or auto-translate. Because reading in French is necessarily harder, necessarily slower, than English, I feel I must bring more of myself to the task.

But what does that mean, *more of myself*? The act of reading feels more physical, more tactile, in French; I am reading not just with my eyes and my brain but also with my breath and my memory, somehow with my body, with my muscles. Sometimes it feels like standing in the middle of an arena surrounded by battle ropes – those rugged, heavy ropes that people lift and lower in a continuous wave to strengthen and build fitness. Each word is a rope, and I must lift it and send it in an explosive ripple to the outer areas of the arena. After a moment the word lights up the dark outskirts of the arena, and I pick up the next rope.

Trees (Part II)

I dislike mixing my breath with someone I have not chosen. With a tree, sure. I am almost certain to receive some oxygen. But with a human?

– Luce Irigaray, 'Ecce Mulier? Fragments'

The Forest Screams

More accurately: the forest shouts. Loud, irregular bellows that come from a clearing about halfway through my hike. The clearing is in the valley, between the river and the gravel road that rises to hug the hillside. There is a grassy area with enormous eucalypts and fallen logs. In spring there are ducklings and tadpoles in the river, trees to climb and blackberry bushes to plunder.

As I approach it always seems as if the tall trees themselves are making the noises. I hear her long before I see her, most days. Sometimes I try to decide on the quality of the noises. Is she shouting or groaning? Bellowing or grunting? She has a chestnut bob, and two gloves that I recognise as microfibre cleaning mitts that have been strapped to her hands because she repeatedly hits herself in the head. Usually she is barefoot, her back to the path, standing near the river. Her carer is usually leaning against a fallen tree watching something on his phone.

The timing of my hikes is irregular but the two of them are often there, which makes me think they must spend six or seven hours in the clearing each day, in this beautiful place, barefoot, shouting.

Outside

The world is beautiful, and outside of it, there is no salvation.

– Albert Camus, 'Le Désert' ('The Desert')

Battle Ropes

The creator of the battle ropes system, John Brookfield, says that 'the key to their effectiveness is that they work each arm independently, eliminating strength imbalances.' With each book I read I learn new words and new expressions – I begin to balance out the nursery rhymes and the words for small animals (*coccinelle, libellule, mille-pattes* – ladybird, dragonfly, millipede). I learn to hold other things.

Blood (Part IV)

We invented so many stories to fill the space in our family history created by my mother's adoption. My mother with her olive skin and blue eyes, her wiry curls and wide smile. Her tenacity. Her face was reconstructed after a crash in her teens; I have never been able to tell how much I resemble her because I'm not sure what she looked like before the accident. The stories we imagined about our ancestry were shaped by the fact that in 1989 my mother's birth mother rejected her appeal for contact. She didn't want to know about us; my mum's letter was an invasion. We took this resistance as a clue – we guessed that she never had a family, that she had issues. It was a one-night stand. My mum had been born to a woman who was raggedy and lonely, who had not been able to care for a daughter, who kept it a secret from the birth father, whom she barely knew. How could we have guessed otherwise? How could we have filled the story with anything other than absences and voids, with unapproachable space?

We could never have imagined the story that eventually unfolded. Far from being the child of a lonely, unstable woman, she was the daughter of a young, unmarried Presbyterian couple who went on to marry and have a son – the man my brother had matched with on the DNA database. My mother had been unwanted not because of a lack of love or ability or family but simply because she had been born *too early*, according to the strictures imposed by religion, before the wedding vows. All the time we were inventing stories, she had had a *full blood brother* who did not know about her. After my own brother reaches out, the response is staggeringly swift. Our all-of-a-sudden-uncle is joyful and generous. We find ourselves gazing at wedding photos, searching for resemblances. They look so respectable, dressed in old-fashioned finery, pressed linen, stiff sateen.

Sans Transition

When I read *La Peste* in French I am shocked by the tenderness and delicacy of the novel. A child smiles at Rieux in the street and I feel as if this moment is all I have ever been looking for in the novel. Although I must have technically read this moment twice already, I feel as if I had never really *read it*. This moment is why I have returned to the book again and again, why I have not been able to accept my dissatisfaction as the final word on the matter.

'I believe that reading in a foreign language is the most intimate way of reading,' Lahiri says. This sense of physicality, of being forced to pay close attention, is part of what makes the act so intimate. Intimacy is *getting close* to something or someone; how do we imagine *being close* without bodies, without touching?

Et soudain, sans transition, l'enfant lui sourit de toutes ses dents. Reading this line in French, I experience it first word by word. 'And' 'suddenly,' 'without' 'transition,' 'the child' 'smiled' 'at' 'him' 'with' 'all' 'of' 'his' 'teeth'. It is only after this swallowing of each word, one after the other, that I can then digest the whole as something closer to 'Suddenly, unexpectedly, the child smiled at him from ear to ear.'

Curious, I go hunting for the version of *The Plague* I read back in that makeshift bookstore in Suffolk. I find the 2002 translation by

Robin Buss. This scene happens just before the end of Part I, when the state of plague is declared: 'Then suddenly, with no stopping halfway, the child gave him a beaming smile.' A nice enough translation. But nothing inside me leaps, crackles, vibrates. Ignites. A child's sudden smile at Rieux, a child on the street smiling in a way that *shows all of his teeth* – that hits me in the place I long to be hit. It disrupts me, makes me feel slightly untethered.

I'm not quite sure what is happening, except that *La Peste* in French allows me access to something stranger, more surprising, more tactile. How I experience the novel is now entirely my own business. Anything I lack, in terms of understanding, is the result of my own failure, my own inadequacies, not something that is being denied to me.

REBELLION

For Camus, it was essential to commit to bearing witness, to promising no false tomorrows, to not passing judgement, and to remaining committed to liberty and solidarity. Camus placed himself 'à mi-distance de la misère et du soleil' – *somewhere between poverty and the sun*. Camus, like Beckett and Nietzsche, also battled with illness: the tuberculosis he had been diagnosed with as a teenager led to periods of illness and confinement for the rest of his life. Camus's response to nihilism involved a sort of sensual, life-embracing vitality that he adopted and promoted. Sea, sex, and sun, perhaps, à la the hedonistic Serge Gainsbourg. If Beckett was sinking, is Camus falling? A sort of intentional, rebellious free-fall?

WHAT'S THE POINT OF LIFE

As a teenager I learned a phrase of my mum's that filled me with admiration and fear. 'What's the point of life if . . .' she'd say, scornfully. 'Mum, you can't afford that,' I'd say breathlessly, as she bought me a white strapless top in an expensive boutique. 'Pfft. What's the point of life if you can't buy a nice top for your daughter?' she'd reply, swiping her credit card and not making eye contact with the sales lady.

VOWELS

An Australian friend of mine in Paris once booked a table for *douze* – twelve – instead of *deux* – two – because she did not know how to pronounce the vowel-cluster 'eux'. It still makes me laugh to think about what she must have looked like upon being shown the long table set for twelve. This is one of the most difficult aspects of learning French as an English speaker. In English, spelling is a famously poor indicator of how a word should sound. In French, *par contre*, you can know how a word is to be pronounced by the way it is spelled. The catch is that if you mispronounce the vowels – if you slip and render one set phoneme in place of another – a French listener can genuinely struggle to comprehend the meaning of the sentence. In English it's different. Vowels are untrustworthy, slippery – the way they are written carries little meaning. New Zealand and South African and Australian and British English are partly differentiated, in speech, by the fact that they render their vowel sounds differently. They are all broadly comprehensible to each other because the assimilation of a word or a sentence in English usually revolves around the sound of the consonants. Modified vowel sounds are like radio static, the brain can fix it, can tune in to that frequency.

196

*

Some French words are themselves merely collections of vowel-sounds, what I like to think of as 'noise words', like 'un', 'eau' or 'y' (*one, water, there*). Because they have no consonants, they do not feel significant enough to me to hold meaning. Each time I say my husband's hometown, 'Rouen', I am surprised to be understood, so far does it sound, to me, from an actual place name, so much does it feel like I am just clearing my throat.

Disobedience

I realized later that there was probably nothing more disobedient than being a comic poet, since no one's ever sure if that's good enough.

– Alice Notley, 'The Poetics of Disobedience'

Rebellion (Part II)

A friend once told me my mum was the first adult she'd ever met who broke the adult alliance in which grown-ups protected one another. After listening to a grim story about my fifteen-year-old friend's father, my mum looked her dead in the eye and said, 'Your father sounds like an arsehole.'

'It filled me with hope,' my friend told me years later. 'He *was* a fucking arsehole.'

DIONYSIAN MOTHERS

Walter Kaufmann dedicated his translation of *The Birth of Tragedy* to his 'Apollonian' grandfather and his 'Dionysian' grandmother. I think of this dedication probably more than I think of any of the contents of *The Birth of Tragedy*. I wonder what his grandmother was like – if she contained both the joy and the terror of the Dionysian. I wonder how society treated her. I wonder what sort of life she lived.

SEEKING RESPITE

In a lecture given at the University of Uppsala in 1957, after being awarded the Nobel Prize in Literature, Camus spoke of Nietzsche, and the period of sadness and solitude that is said to have marked the period of his life after his falling out with two of his closest friends and companions from his time in Sorrento, Paul Rée and Lou Salomé. Camus explained that apparently Nietzsche felt 'both crushed and elevated by the prospect of the enormity of the work that was his alone to accomplish', a sentiment that is echoed mournfully by Nietzsche's Zarathustra in *Thus Spoke Zarathustra*. During this period, Nietzsche, Camus says, walked at night 'through the mountains that dominate the Gulf of Genoa, lighting huge bonfires of leaves and branches and watching them burn', and goes on to tell his audience:

> I have often dreamt of these fires, and I have imagined placing before them certain artists, certain artworks, to test their worth . . . One may wish, as I do, for a gentler flame, for respite, for the break conducive to daydreaming. But perhaps there is no other peace for an artist than that which can be found in the heat of

combat. Let us seek instead respite where it can be found, and by that I mean, in the heart of the battle.

Abîmer

With each book I read in French, I lock away a new piece of vocabulary. With *L'Étranger* it is *huissier*, meaning bailiff. With Irigaray's *Amante Marine* I learn *abîme*, abyss. This word is connected to a word I already know, *abîmer* (Mamie Solange telling my children: 'Il faut pas abîmer les choses!' *Don't damage things!*) These ideas, in French, are netted together, the idea of the abyss, and the idea of damage – or rather, of tearing, ripping something apart – I must have first learned the word in relation to fabric, because it is torn fabric I picture when I hear the word *abîmer*. Once I learn this, it is hard to unhook the abyss from this idea of ruin, of destruction.

The Sun (Part II)

Camus said that the only true function of man, born into an absurd world, is to live, be aware of one's life, one's revolt, one's freedom. He said that if the only solution to the human dilemma is death, then we are on the wrong road. The right track is the one that leads to life, to the sunlight . . . The track he followed led into the sunlight in being that one devoted to making, with our frail powers and our absurd material, something which had not existed in life until we had made it.

– William Faulkner, Obituary for Albert Camus

DÉMÉNAGEMENT

Déménagement – 'moving house' – is constructed around the word *ménage*, meaning household. I think of the prefix 'dé' functioning here with the same ferocity as it does in words like 'decapitate' or 'defenestrate'. *Déménager* – to unhome, unhouse. To eject oneself, forcefully, from the household, or domicile. A *femme de ménage* is a cleaning lady, *faire le ménage* means to do the housework, and *ménage-a-trois*, familiar to English speakers as another term for three-some, is literally 'a household of three'. I'll let you guess which term I use most frequently.

THE ARENA OF THE UNWELL (PART II)

It's difficult to do extensive research into Nietzsche without coming up, again and again, against his illnesses. He was 'perpetually sick', claiming that he felt good 'at best one day in ten'. In typical Nietzschean fashion, the philosopher also celebrated his sickness, insisting that his illness had freed him from his professional duties, rendering him too unwell to teach or to read. It also released him from his sense of fidelity to his forebears in the discipline of philology:

Sickness *detached me slowly*: it spared me any break, any violent and offensive step . . . My sickness also gave me the right to change all my habits completely; it permitted, it *commanded* me to forget; it bestowed on me the necessity of lying still, of leisure, of waiting and being patient . . . That nethermost self which had, as it were, been buried and grown silent under the continual pressure of having to listen to other selves (and that is after all what reading means) awakened slowly, shyly, dubiously – but eventually it spoke again.

Nietzsche recovered himself and his own voice in this sickness that commanded him to stop, to convalesce, to forget. He claimed that his illness liberated him – the 'nethermost self' that had been buried awoke and spoke – or perhaps roared. This reminds me of the lion again, the lion – as Nietzsche tells us in *Thus Spoke Zarathustra* – which is needed for the 'creation of freedom for oneself and a sacred "No" even to duty', turning ferociously upon all that it had been taught, all that it had learned, been smothered by. The lion turns and destroys obligation, duty, fidelity to knowledge and to scripture. But the transformation is not complete – the lion is not enlightened. I cannot move past the lion, cannot reject and refuse all of my duties; I still have no interest in becoming 'the child', which Nietzsche claims is able to forget, move forward, uttering the 'sacred Yes' and creating anew.

But what does Nietzsche know about children? Children never forget.

THE ISLAND, REVISITED

My daughter wants to talk about the island. 'Do you remember,' she says breathlessly, 'the house on the hill with the figs?' We are driving to the beach, it is 41 degrees at sunset. I feel trapped inside an oven of heat. 'Yes,' I reply, turning off the music, and she recounts the walk down the mountain to the bay, the afternoon we swam out to a little island, the crustaceans we found, the water as it sparkled in the bright sun. I park the car and breathe in the dunes, the saltbush, the flat surface of the water. My son is afraid of stingrays hidden beneath the sand. The wind is hot. We collapse into the cool salt water and my son starts a song called 'Clap clap clap catch', following me relentlessly through the water, afraid to be alone. I can still hear him when I dive away, down towards the deep.

*

201

The island. A last effort. The islet. The shore facing the open sea is jagged with creeks. One could live there, perhaps happy, if life was a possible thing, but nobody lives there.

– Samuel Beckett, *Malone Dies*

DÉMÉNAGEMENT (PART II)

My friend who left her husband buys a print for her new apartment. It arrives framed and she hangs it immediately. It is a picture of two women sunbathing topless on the Amalfi Coast, burnt orange sunshades pulled down over their faces so that only their smooth brown bodies are visible, reclining luxuriously on mustard yellow towels. Shoes have been kicked off. The entire scene is aspirational, glamorous. It is easy to covet – those bodies, that sun, a life in which you might be confident enough to have a tan that indicates days, weeks, perhaps half a lifetime, of topless sunbathing. The shadows are rich and sharp. The woman on the left is wearing a tiny black bikini bottom and the one on the right a tangerine-coloured one-piece that has been pulled down to expose her breasts – as if sunning her breasts is more important than anything else. As if her only job today is to get some sun on her breasts – if all else fails, at least she has tanned her breasts.

I get stuck in my writing because I keep looking at bikinis online. Triangle hipster cobalt. Arthouse side-tie high-waisted. Strapless. Hawaiian. Sea-dive green.

Rebellion (Part III)

Must we say 'no' in the name of something? Can't we say 'no', like my friend, and her marriage, in the name of nothing?

Lost in the Wind

I now think that if literature written by women wants to have its own writing of truth, the work of each of us is needed . . . Against the bad language that historically doesn't provide a welcome for our truth, we have to confuse, fuse our talents, not a line should be lost in the wind.

— Elena Ferrante, *In the Margins*

Resistance

The human condition: to be filled with insatiable longing, yearning, awareness of lack and catastrophic desire for a higher purpose, some sort of meaning – and to be confronted with the absolute stillness and silence of a universe that will not answer, that will not offer solace. We exist in that space, between longing and silence. According to Camus, we should resist trying to resolve – we should learn to tolerate – the tensions and dilemmas inherent in life. We must resist our potent and vociferous need for meaning, purpose, unity, cohesion.

Women who Hike . . .

. . . or who walked a lot, or wrote about walking, or conducted their reportage on the streets, on their feet: Virginia Woolf, Olivia Laing,

Cheryl Strayed, Lauren Elkin, Robyn Davidson, George Sand, Sophie Calle, Martha Gellhorn, Rebecca Solnit.

FREEDOM (PART III)

The question, for those who cannot live without art and all that it signifies, is only to know how, despite the spouters of countless ideologies (so many churches, such loneliness!), the strange liberty of creation remains possible.

– Albert Camus, 'Discours de Suède' ('Nobel Prize Speeches')

MOVEMENT

If being stuck is a type of nihilism, then is movement – even if only pacing the cage or the prison you find yourself in – the opposite of nihilism? I clock Camus's preoccupation with the sensual, although I'm not quite sure what to do with it until a friend says she thinks I should read *The Spell of the Sensuous: Perception and Language in a More-than-Human World* by David Abram. Okay, I think. I've given up trying to swat books away. Abram opens the book like this:

Late one evening, I stepped out of my little hut in the rice paddies of eastern Bali and found myself falling through space. Over my head the black sky was rippling with stars, densely clustered in some regions, almost blocking out the darkness between them, and loosely scattered in other areas, pulsing and beckoning to each other. Behind them all streamed the great river of light with its several tributaries. Yet the Milky Way churned beneath me as well, for my hut was set in the middle of a large patchwork of rice paddies, separated from each other by narrow two-foot-high

204

dikes, and these paddies were all filled with water. The surface of these pools, by day, reflected perfectly the blue sky, a reflection broken only by the thin, bright green tips of new rice. But by night, the stars themselves glimmered from the surface of the paddies, and the river of light whirled through the darkness underfoot as well as above; there seemed no ground in front of my feet, only the abyss of star-studded space falling away forever.

– David Abram, *The Spell of the Sensuous*

What's the Point of Life (Part II)

What's the point of life if you can't . . .? There's no answer to this question. It's a Dionysian question, a question designed to unmask us, to reveal the delusions we live by. *Society can only survive if it acknowledges the fundamental violence at the heart of the polis*, I have written in the margins of my notes from the symposium on blood. My mother's approach to life is an attack on the hegemony of reason and control. There is no answer because the premise of the question is that *there is no point*, or at least no point that has greater value than whatever we assign to this moment, this act. It's a hedonistic phrase that refutes denial, that embraces desire. It doesn't make sense to say *What's the point of life if you can't litter.* Or, *What's the point of life if you can't kick puppies.* It works, however, if completed with assertions like *if you can't have a smoke on your birthday*, or *if you can't have cake for breakfast.* It mocks denial. It's beautiful; it's dangerous. It is as unruly and rebellious as my mother.

The Sun (Part III)

In the young light of the sun, winter will be dry. August extinguishes the colours in the lands of the sun, but the cold shines, the sky is blue with snow. Dark summers, golden winters: true strength has two faces.

– Albert Camus, *La Postérité du Soleil* (*The Posterity of the Sun*)

Blood (Part V)

It is destabilising to feel, all at once, something firm beneath your feet after a lifetime of unknowns. Like sailors whose sea legs make them unsteady on land. *Mal de débarquement*, it is called, the sense that the land is rolling after you arrive ashore. The story my mother has been searching for turns out to be so whole, so ordinary. She is so different to the people in the photographs, the Presbyterian family ruled by a religion that refused to raise her. She was forged by absence. If she'd grown up with the family in the photographs, she wouldn't be the same. I wouldn't be the same. The news of her family unravels her; she sobs all day. I don't know how to help. 'You can't do anything about her sadness,' my dad tells me on the phone. 'You've just got to let her have it.' When the evening comes, anger nestles in with it, and I yell at everyone before pulling on my crumpled running clothes and heading out into the night. I run through the dark streets fuelled by rage. I hate everyone, I hate everything. The night is cold and dark, and I want to run forever. By the next morning Mum has recovered, and it is my turn to sob on the phone. My fear of saying the wrong thing turns into saying everything, hoping something will be right. What I can't get over is how *unfragmented* the story is – it's not about lost love or broken promises, a jigsaw in a thousand pieces. How *whole* their family is breaks me. Mum has a keen sense of the betrayal her younger brother might feel. 'At least I always knew I was adopted, I knew I had another family,' she says. 'He had no idea.' The absence she had lived with her whole life is suddenly shared – she was a gap in his life, a relationship that had been denied him. She knows what this is like, how devastating it must feel.

Hiking (Part II)

Is it even really hiking, what I am doing? Or is it just another version of Kant's mechanical strolls throughout his hometown of Königsberg? Nietzsche called Kant a nihilist, too, positioning him against *ikigai*, or the idea of being internally motivated or 'called' by our own desires or instincts:

> This nihilist with his Christian dogmatic entrails considered pleasure an *objection*. What could destroy us more quickly than working, thinking, and feeling without any inner necessity, without any deeply personal choice, without pleasure – as an automaton of 'duty'? This is the very recipe for decadence, even for idiocy. Kant became an idiot.

Blood (Part VI)

Access blood, access the truth . . . After the talk on Odysseus, I stalk through the rest of the symposium on high alert, no longer tired or listless. After everything my blood has revealed, I want to learn how to measure its value, determine its validity. I take obsessive notes about blood and delirium, about blood in poetry of the English Civil War, and the metaphorical value of blood as passion, vitality, and guilt. The final speaker of the day talks about blood donations and transfusion services. There is no viable synthetic substitute for blood, or plasma, which means it has been harvested in poorer countries like Haiti to supply wealthier nations like the United States with the necessary quotas for transfusions. Blood has become another tool in the neoliberal catastrophe. I cannot quite reconcile this with my search, and it haunts me: bleeding the life out of the disenfranchised and disempowered to supply literal life and vitality to the wealthier, luckier, more powerful. Is this, then, the meaning of blood? That which sustains life, that which is not our own, but tradeable, exchangeable, that which can be stolen? Is it blood that is the chaos at the heart of the polis?

Freedom (Part IV)

When I read *On Freedom* by Maggie Nelson, I get a little closer to understanding what I'm doing with the Nietzschean-sobriety-pact. I think I'm after what Nelson calls 'a kind of freedom one can't go at or for directly, by an act of will, but must be accessed indirectly, through renunciation, undoneness, abandonment . . . It's more of a subtraction, by which one touches a certain bareness, the bareness of one's own bare life.'

Lost in the Wind (Part II)

This is precisely what happens to our efforts to write: the words are ready *para formar el libro*, says María Guerra, and yet they won't stay in the form, they overflow the margins, get lost in the wind.

– Elena Ferrante, *In the Margins*

Blood (Part VII)

For most of my life I believed I was in charge of my own vitality and feeling lifeless had nothing to do with my blood – that it was psychological, or spiritual, an emotional imbalance. As if I were not at the mercy of that which flowed through my veins, as though I could continue if it drained out of me, believing in another source of vigour. Being forced to respect the necessary health of the lingua franca of my body made me healthier, and heartier. But there is an obvious limit to what the blood knows, or holds. My mother's blood did not shape her. We did not find a family of wild Nietzscheans, hedonistic and rebellious and swamped in credit card debt. The woman who raised me taught me how to determine myself in a void, unfettered by expectation or predisposition. Blood talks, but ultimately it can only tell you what it knows. Blood can tell you that you are sick, but it cannot tell you who you are.

Noticing

In one of Nancy Lemann's short stories a man tells the narrator that driving into a giant storm will be good for her soul. The narrator must drive into the storm across 'the longest bridge in the world', which I keep misreading as 'the loneliest bridge in the world' because that's the texture of this moment – this man sending her away from his house and into the storm, telling her it will be good for her soul. The narrator records this in her 'Diary of Remorse', as she calls it, and follows it with, 'Because fear is good for the soul? The way despair can make you notice things more? That is the whole point of everything – to notice things more.'

I think about this a lot, about *despair making you notice more,* about *the whole point of everything.*

THE SUN (PART IV)

My mother was devoted to tanning. She would do her outdoor chores in a bikini top and denim shorts: weeding the garden, hanging out laundry, refurbishing old furniture she had found. Once when we were teenagers my sister brought some friends home unexpectedly and our mother was mowing the lawn of our secluded valley property completely topless. My sister was horrified, and my mother admonished her for being a prude, laughing, before heading inside to grab a cotton singlet.

> Poverty . . . was never a source of unhappiness for me: sunlight spread its riches. It even enlightened my rebellions. Poverty stopped me from believing that all was well under the sun, and in history. The sun taught me that history isn't everything.
>
> — Albert Camus, *Essais* (*Essays*)

THE ISLAND, REVISITED (PART II)

To get to the island we have to hitch a ride on a small motorboat. There is a short walk up the mountain to the villa when we arrive. The villa is designed to be breezy and open, but the weather is suffocatingly hot and the wind is already threatening damage, so we close all of the windows and doors and wonder how brutal the typhoon will prove.

I am not used to destructive wind, the type that flattens trees and smashes houses. The evening has an eerie, foreign romance to it. After the children fall asleep, we drink beer and whiskey and I get into an argument with one of our new friends. Our friend is drunk and loses his way easily. He is drinking red wine and his thinking is sloppy – his laughing, argumentative drunkenness is familiar to me, almost pleasant. The argument even ends the way most of the arguments in my family end – with him patting me on the shoulder and telling me that he needs to take a piss. The disagreement, vaguely, is about Ecclesiastes and whether there is any purpose in life – I quote something my dad had said to me once and our friend looks startled. 'Hang on – he said what?' 'He said the journey into nihilism was interesting, but it's the trip back that really counts.'

The next morning our friend does not even have a hangover. He's hauling the children up the mountain to raid a fig tree; my son is lolloping after him, yelling about a cricket he has found. I sit on the balcony and try to read but feel curiously unbuckled, as if a chasm has opened in my life and I am about to fall into it.

Essaying

Nietzsche instructs us to make of ourselves a work of art, but I'm beginning to feel that art is not something that can be made – it can only be attempted. Attempting, attempting, attempting to be art, to make art, to make oneself a work of art . . . To access the art that one always has been?

Ecriture Séduisante (Part III)

What leads to a true understanding of Nietzsche is precisely of that which the seductive allurements of his writings appear to promise: not the acceptance of definitive pronouncements, taken to convey the final and indefeasible truth, but rather the sustained effort in which we continue to question, listen to other contentions, and maintain the tension of possibilities.

– Karl Jasper

Experiment (Part II)

Ultimately, French leads me nowhere productive: it contains no danger, or none that I am willing to engage with. French is not a deep, profound lake I am swimming across with my heart in my mouth; French is a wading pool, warm from the heat of the summer sun, that I am lounging in as I splash water at my young children. I do not mean to imply that French is not . . . impossible, I don't mean to claim any kind of lazy mastery. It is simply not a solitary elsewhere I can engage with; it is not an *ailleurs*. French does not scare me, and therefore cannot inspire me.

French is not turning inward: French is not the fertile abyss. It never will be. I am not looking for another type of danger, another kind of creative inspiration, a way of stripping down and stepping back from mastery and ease. Writing still scares me. When I write, my skin feels like it is on fire. I feel as if I am trying to turn myself inside out to write with my sinew and gizzards and gore. Back in that black leotard with my head in a lion's maw. To return to Nietzsche's *feeling of living*: it is in writing and leaving that my feeling of living is the greatest. As I can no longer leave, the voiceless abyss that speaks to me of my fate urges me to write, write, write. But the question remains: how to work in suspension, how to use a cage with freedom?

Danger

For – believe me – the secret for harvesting from existence the greatest fruitfulness and the greatest enjoyment is – *to live dangerously!*

– Friedrich Nietzsche, *The Gay Science*

For Jhumpa Lahiri, the security of English does not offer any sense of marvel or wonder – in Italian the desperate striving, the impossibility of mastery, is a necessary, inexplicable but essential impulse. 'From the creative point of view there is nothing so dangerous as security,' Lahiri writes. And later, paraphrasing Fuentes: 'an awareness of impossibility is central to the creative impulse'.

WAYFARERS ALL (PART VI)

And then, before we knew it, we were at the end of 'Wayfarers All' and back to the adventures of the boastful, hilarious Toad, to my son's delight. The chapter ends with the Mole finally finding the answer to help the Water Rat move past his ennui, his debilitating and confusing longing to travel:

> Presently the tactful Mole slipped away and returned with a pencil and a few half-sheets of paper, which he placed on the table at his friend's elbow.
> 'It's quite a long time since you did any poetry,' he remarked.

THE BLISSFUL ISLES

I have been raging against this cage, these circumstances, but I was the one who left Shiraishi Island and returned to my hometown, and *willingly so*. I dug myself into this crevasse. It's true that once I was back the sky became silent and the borders became impassable and there was no escape, the door was locked: but I had willingly taken the overnight route that led away from my Blissful Isles, I had chosen to leave before the earth shook and made return impossible.

The wind rises, *il faut tenter de vivre* . . .

213

BODIES (PART II)

The immortality of the soul, it's true, preoccupies many great minds. But that is because they refuse, before having exhausted its sap, the only truth given to them, and that is the body. Because the body does not trouble them, or, at least, they know the only solution it proposes: the body is a truth that must decay, and, as such, assumes a bitterness and a nobility that they do not dare to face. Great minds prefer poetry, because it speaks of the soul. Yes, I am playing with words. But it is understood as well that by truth I wish only to consecrate a higher poetry . . . the clear-sighted protest of man thrown upon an earth on which the splendor and the light speak to him relentlessly of a God that does not exist.

– Albert Camus, 'Le Désert', ('The Desert')

FAILURE

Did I mean it when I said I left Shiraishi Island, *and willingly so?* I know when I left Japan I felt a terrible sense of failure. The experiment had failed. I had not been remade, rewired, reinvented. And in retrospect *of course* the experiment failed. What a wild idea it had been! As if I could hold on to my husband and children and also disappear, as if I could remain a devoted mother and partner and *burn everything else down.* And yet that, I think, is what I had hoped for – to be split open and emerge as a monster from a pupae, but a monster that my children would still call *Maman.* Leaving Japan was the right choice for everyone in the family except for me; our return was a decision from which I never recovered.

BODIES (PART III)

Secretly I know I began this project of looking into Nietzsche and exploring his concept of nihilism and revaluation expecting to be convinced, as I had been, in Paris, in my twenties, of the urgency, primacy, and value of a life devoted to poetry, literature and artistry. I thought I'd hunt around for evidence – evidence I was confident I would find – of poetry and literature as *privileged sites of resistance to nihilism*. I'd gone back hungry, but also cocky – I knew my deficit, knew the prescription, was confident of the efficacy of the infusion I would receive.

It was humbling, then, to find myself so persistently reminded of the way that Nietzsche's philosophy, Beckett's writings and Camus' reflections position themselves against answers, conviction, certitude. Instead of poetry, I find myself increasingly preoccupied with something I learned in giving birth to my children, something I did not think I needed to learn again: the *inescapable parameters* and *irrefutable truth* of the body. I am surprised to find these famous nihilists celebrating the body's intelligence, physical robustness, health, vivacity, although in Beckett's case it is a sort of reverse celebration, the misery of the body in states of decline. 'You say "I" and you are proud of this word. But greater than this – although you will not believe in it – is your body and its great intelligence, which does not say "I" but performs "I",' writes Nietzsche in *Thus Spoke Zarathustra*. It is the body I find again and again as the rebellion, against false hope, against empty faith, against intellectual posturing. But what does it mean? Is the body the cage? Is the body the site of resistance to nihilism? Can it be both?

PREOCCUPATION

Sometimes it is impossible to tell what is the candle and what is the script that is being illuminated, what is the nail, what is the hammer. I cannot tell if I keep noticing the preoccupation that Nietzsche, Beckett, and Camus have with *the body* as a 'privileged site of resistance to nihilism' or if this is merely my own preoccupation. I cannot tell if that is what is right for me to find in the text at this point in my life, after carrying and giving birth to two children, struggling through a debilitating iron deficiency, approaching middle age with a bad neck – if when we read texts we reach each time for a different candle, or hold that candle to different parts of our minds. And I cannot tell if this is a preoccupation because I am *sick of this pasty, feeble flesh* or because I want to justify the leopard-print push-up triangle bikini I've found online.

'I think I need to buy a bikini for my research,' I tell my husband, and he laughs at me. I text a friend. *I told Guillaume I needed to buy a bikini for my research and he laughed at me.*

Outrageous, she replies. *Who is he to question the creative process?*

REPETITION

'If that which has been flung were to remain out of danger, it would not have been ventured . . .' *The ventured is unprotected but the venture is its security.*

POSTSCRIPTS

In a crowded department store, searching for a gift for my daughter, I come across a strange vermillion makeup brush, designed to be held in the palm and divided into four distinct sections, like the lobes of a maple leaf, or the fat petals of a cherry blossom. 'Can you explain this to me?' I ask a young sales attendant, who cannot. It is expensive; I rarely wear makeup. Despite its expense, despite not needing it (because of its expense? because it is unnecessary?) I say, 'I'm going to take it,' and the sales attendant nods in astonishment. 'It called to me,' I tell her idiotically, but her flawless face offers no reaction.

Riding home I veer left suddenly and take the route I used to take to drive my son to his childcare centre, set in the middle of a eucalyptus forest. It is a route I have often run over the years, and as I take the roundabout at the top of the hill I glance at the house there, a beautiful cottage tucked into the landscape and surrounded by Japanese maples and small oak trees, painted a dry, blue-gum grey with white window frames. I remember the moment I fell in love with this house. It was during the pandemic; I was on one of my restless, roaming runs around the neighbourhood, and as I looked up at the house I glimpsed, through a window, an old-fashioned electric fan sitting on a heavy wooden desk. I imagined the grace of working inside such a beautiful piece of architecture, the view over the arboretum that sprawls down the mountainside from the forest and the fields above. I had a shock of desire for something that felt aesthetic, unobtainable, local.

As I pass the house on my motorbike, balancing against the curve of the roundabout, the rage of red and orange autumn leaves and the quiet grandeur of the house smack up against me, as if I had ploughed into them. I realise in that moment, like a revelation, that the makeup brush is an attempt to buy this, somehow, an attempt to buy autumn, to buy an elegant house of my own in which to write, to buy the fuchsia of the flowers that cling to the otherwise bare branches of the unknown trees in the arboretum.

Or rather I realise something more clearly along the lines of *This is what you truly want.* I hear this realisation *with my heart.* I know this is a cliché; I cannot not write that sentence. I cannot not write it because how does one argue with the heart? With the limbs, the organs, the wide highways of veins and tendons? This so-deep-body-knowing. Like an unexpected epiphany, like a physical impact, that reshapes you. Or reminds you. That you are just paper, just petals, just mist. Dispersible. That longing is what makes you. That the range of your human experience is every shape of the moon, waxing through waning, full moon and no moon, moon in the dawn light, in the midday sky.

Ghost Flowers

When I arrive home from the department store, I do not unpack the makeup brush from its elegant black cardboard packaging. I do not cup the beautiful rounded base in the palm of my hand, gently graze my jawline with the soft red polishing brush. But I do look up the translation of its name into English: *hanatsubaki hake.* I know 'hana' to be the word for flower, and 'baki' reminds me of the word for 'ghost' – *obake. Ghost flowers*, I think. I discover that *tsubaki* means 'camellia'. I've written about Japanese camellias before, the ones that hung heavy over the path behind the apartment block and the sports fields, on the route to the library and along the river. I hunt back through street view to find that path I used to walk, the track I took when it was raining and my heart was breaking at the thought of leaving Japan. When I locate the long row of flowers that run along the path I'm astonished at how high the hedge is, the mixture of white and pink, how small the flowers. I remember them being red, spread open with rain. I take screen grabs, I search online. I discover the flowers are not *tsubaki* but *kyōchikutō*, 'oleanders'. That would explain my memory of their wet, heavy fragrance, the way I almost wanted to laugh as I passed under them, their shameless riot of colour and perfume seeming to mock my aching heart, my total despair.

REPETITION (PART II)

It is an excellent thing to express a thing consecutively in two ways, and thus provide it with a right and a left foot. Truth can stand indeed on one leg, but with two she will walk and complete her journey.

— Nietzsche, *The Wanderer and His Shadow*

THE DULL BITS

A writer I admire once asked me about making peace with the longing-for-elsewhere, living with the wrenching sacrifice of offering your children *normality* and *stability* in exchange for your own adventure, your own wild path. She knows, she said, so many women living with this particular ache. I prevaricated; told her the story of deciding to leave Japan. 'My husband and I went to a restaurant we'd been told about – a strange, chaotic café up on a hill, full of plants and wood; everything looked handmade, including the cutlery and the water mugs, and the menu was vegetarian – I remember it so clearly because we only went there once, just for this lunch, for this particular conversation, one we had been avoiding. And we sat and we ordered and we ate and we went through each member of the family and we talked about whether it would be better for them to stay in Japan, or return to Australia. We started with my daughter, and then discussed my son, and then we talked about my husband, and by the time we got to me, it didn't matter what I wanted. What I wanted, or needed, was irrelevant – 75% of the family needed to return to Australia. It didn't matter how alive I felt, how secure, how myself – three quarters of the family needed to leave. I am only one quarter. I am only 25%.' 'You should write that,' the writer said intently. 'You should replace the dull bits with that story.' Although I love this suggestion, I've come to realise I cannot replace the dull bits; that's part of the point, I think. Of this. Of me. Of longing.

THE SOURCE

Each artist therefore carries deep within themselves a unique source, which nourishes during their lifetime what they are, and what they say. When the source has dried up, little by little their work shrivels, and cracks. These are the barren plains of art that the invisible current no longer irrigates . . . For me, I know that my source is . . . in this world of poverty and sunlight that I lived in for a long time, the memory of which still now protects me from the opposing dangers that threaten every artist: resentment, and satisfaction.

– Albert Camus, 'Préface', *L'Envers et L'Endroit*,
(*The Wrong Side and the Right Side*)

HANATSUBAKI HAKE

I look up the store's return policy. I place the *hanatsubaki hake* in the heavy cardboard bag it came in. I am sad that I cannot buy what is missing. I am angry that polishing my face with this petal brush will not bring me any closer to *what I truly want*. I am wild with the idea that *what I truly want* is not an object, not even a house, but rather an instinct, a suspicion, a fleeting sense of potential force, of adventure, of surprise. What I want is so difficult to articulate, it feels beyond the words I have. It is not that I long for things that no longer exist; more like I long for things I do not yet know. Not 'far-ache', or *fernweh*, not the *unheimlich*, or 'uncanny', it is not things that are strangely familiar, it is not nostalgia, it is not return, or being unable to return, or misremembering, or too-visceral remembering. It is the potent desire, still, for something utterly unexpected, for the freefall of being knocked clean out of myself in a foreign city by a careening motorbike full of hoodlums early in the evening on the way to a bar to meet friends. On a night when I anticipated something different, nothing, everything.

POSTSCRIPTS (PART II)

A prose poem I wrote on my first writing retreat, many years ago, goes like this:

All you do is push ups and wind sprints and cobra poses. You're not here to run, you're here to write, but each morning the forest pulls you in, the track drags you up, and the view from the crest contains so many different shades of light. You run like a restless athlete, recovering from an old injury, you run like you are being rehabilitated. The musicians play in their cottage while you run, you can hear the piano shaking. You find the painter's lipstick in the woods where she sits all day with her canvas. But you – you are in hiding, and you know it. So you run, as if you can run out of it, as if you can outrun it, as if you can just sweat it out of you and towel it off and never ever hear that sweet ache of a voice in your heart ever again.

That sweet ache of a voice. That's the one I heard, tilting into the roundabout that afternoon.

(Don't Be So) Restless

There are things restless women do. You know what I mean. Have affairs. Drink heavily. Run away. I've got a thing for narratives about mothers who leave – I love, in particular, Anne Tyler's *Ladder of Years* and her restless narrator who just keeps walking one morning, along the beach, and eventually starts a new life for herself in a town far from her husband and grown children. But none of those seem like real options to me, for me – or rather, perhaps, they feel like blueprint options, social conditioning options, red pill/blue pill options. What if I want to take the amber pill, the emerald pill, the violet, golden, opalescent pill? What if I want another way out? What if the restlessness can point elsewhere, or propel me elsewhere, if only I can hold onto it, and not get distracted with impossible love affairs, the lure of whiskey, running away, moving overseas, the tug of the promise of false escape?

The Abyss Speaks

There is another layer to the voice – the more I think about it, the more I realise it was making a more complex statement than *This is what you truly want*. I'm trying to translate from a wordless place, a felt place, a heart-voice that beats, rather than speaks. It wasn't just *This is what you truly want*. More like *This is getting in the way*. Or, *Please accept that what you want is otherwise*. And also, *This ache cannot be silenced*. The voice was kind of emphatic, it was kind of enormous. I know I could also translate the voice in another way, a more pointed way. Because it was also saying, *Who the fuck do you think you are trying to fool?* It was also saying, *This is a betrayal.* It was saying, *Do you think this ache can be silenced by a fucking makeup brush in the shape of a flower?* It was also saying, *Please stop being so sad and so small you think you can spend $65 and avoid the terrible strength of your own desire.* It was like living a haiku. I felt the beauty and regret of the moment in equal measure, aware of the ephemeral nature of all that matters, and the cost of everything superficial and pointless. I said to the voice, I replied almost immediately, *Hey, calm down. It's not that important to me. It's just a stupid makeup brush. I'll return it if that is the right thing to do. I'll return it. Don't be afraid.*

The makeup brush is in its sharp little box in the handsome packaging ready to be returned, but I have not returned it yet. Whether I return it seems now beside the point, although I suspect I will, as some sort of act of voodoo to assuage that voice, to assure it that I will not be side-tracked from my real purpose, my real desire. There is no point to owning it, I tell myself; whatever magic it held has dispersed. (Or, a part of me whispers, the magic has run its course, the magic was triggered by the sight of the brush, the purchase of the brush, I was meant to buy it because I was meant to regret it – because regret would trigger a deeper engagement with all that I lack?) Is the *hanatsubaki hake* now an object I will never use but instead keep on my desk like a little red lantern I can raise against the night-time of my own despair? As a pretty symbol of the impossibility of ever making peace with what I long for?

POSTSCRIPTS (PART III)

I know I will continue to give into these lures, I will keep falling for ersatz pleasures, satisfactions. Makeup brushes. Dresses. Bikinis. I'm vulnerable to things that feel like they might contain the tiniest taste of escape. But I'm trying to establish a sort of pact with myself that if I notice I am doing it, I will *try to resist*. I'll keep running into the storm, allow the haiku to unfold. I will remain faithful, committed to seeking that which cannot be bought, cannot be held, and may never be found. Accepting that I seek what I cannot name or know, because what I seek is what I do not know and have never named. I'm not even looking to name, to know. Just to be in it. To be *hors d'ici, hors de maintenant*. 'Outside of here, outside of now.'

Voices Cited

The translations from *Thus Spoke Zarathustra* by Friedrich Nietzsche used throughout this book are by R. J. Hollingdale, published by Penguin Classics. Copyright © R. J. Hollingdale, 1961, 1969. Reprinted by permission of Penguin Books Limited. Translations of Nietzsche's *Human, All Too Human, The Gay Science* and *Beyond Good and Evil* are reproduced with permission from Cambridge University Press via PlsClear.

Christian Bök's *Eunoia* has been excerpted with the kind permission of the author.

Suji Kwock Kim's poem, 'Monologue for an Onion', from *Notes From the Divided Country*, 2003, has been reproduced with the permission of Louisiana State University Press.

Sabrina Orah Mark's work, including *The Babies*, has been excerpted with the kind permission of the author.

Quotations from Natalia Ginzburg's *Little Virtues*, translated by Dick Davis, have been reproduced with the permission of Edizione Einaudi and Daunt Books.

Quotations from *In Other Words* © Jhumpa Lahiri, translated by Ann Goldstein, 2015, are reproduced with the permission of Bloomsbury Publishing Plc.

The Journey Out of Nihilism

'Your freedom as a writer . . .' Annie Dillard, *The Writing Life*, HarperCollins, New York, NY, 2013, p. 11.

'Speech that is indistinguishable from silence . . .' Stanley Rosen, *Nihilism: A Philosophical Essay*, Yale University Press, New Haven, CT, 1969, p. xix.

'Retreat? No! I want to go on an advance!' is a comment made by Arundhati Roy in an interview with Charlotte Sinclair, 'Why happiness is a radical act', *British Vogue*, 27 July 2017, <www.vogue.co.uk/article/arundhati-roy-interview>.

'You don't have to be a poet . . .' Olivia Laing, *To the River: a Journey Beneath the Surface*, Canongate, Edinburgh, UK, 2011, p. 188.

'Indeed, at hearing the news . . .' Friedrich Nietzsche, trans. Josefine Nauckhoff, *The Gay Science: With a Prelude in German Rhymes and an Appendix of Songs*, Book Four [Fragment 343], Cambridge University Press, Cambridge, UK, 2001, p. 199.

'. . . but to create itself freedom . . .' Friedrich Nietzsche's *Thus Spoke Zarathustra*, trans. R. J. Hollingdale, Penguin Books, London, UK, 2003, p. 55.

'The great liberation comes for those who are thus fettered . . .' Friedrich Nietzsche, trans. R. J. Hollingdale, *Human, All Too Human: A Book for free Spirits*, Cambridge University Press, Cambridge, UK, 2018, [Preface, Fragment 3], p. 7.

'. . . a rebellious, arbitrary, volcanically erupting desire for travel . . .' Nietzsche, trans. Hollingdale, *Human, All Too Human*, [Preface, Fragment 3], p. 7.

'Nihilism does not only contemplate . . .' Friedrich Nietzsche, trans. Walter Kaufmann and R. J. Hollingdale, *The Will to Power*, Book 1: European Nihilism [Fragment 24], Vintage Books, New York, NY, 1968, p. 18.

'Are poems written on such themes . . .' Yoshida Kenkō, trans. Donald Keene, *Essays in Idleness*, Tuttle, North Clarendon, VT, 1981, [Fragment 137], p. 115.

'a type of involuntary . . .' Friedrich Nietzsche, trans. Judith Norman, *Beyond Good and Evil: Prelude to a Philosophy of the Future*, Cambridge University Press, Cambridge, UK, 2002, [Fragment 6], p. 8.

'As a nonfiction writer you must get on the plane' William Zinsser, 'A Writer's Decisions' in *On Writing Well*, HarperCollins, New York, NY, 1998, p. 285.

'the knowability of things . . .' Nietzsche, trans. Hollingdale, *Daybreak* [Fragment 547] in *A Nietzsche Reader*, pp. 33–34.

'Look at you, chopping and weeping . . .' Suji Kwock Kim, 'Monologue for an Onion' in *Notes from the Divided Country*, Louisiana State University Press, Baton Rouge, LA, 2003, pp. 51–52.

'The same feeling of not belonging . . .' Emil Cioran, trans. Richard Howard, *The Trouble with Being Born*, Penguin Random House, London, UK, 2020, p. 22.

Anne Lamott explaining Beckett's famous nihilism is a reference to Lamott's *Bird by Bird: some instructions on writing and life*, Scribe Publications, Melbourne, 2019, p. 200: 'The redemption in Beckett is so small: in the second act of *Waiting for Godot*, the barren dying twig of a tree has put out a leaf. Just one leaf. It's not much; still Beckett didn't commit suicide. He wrote.'

'There is not a steel divider that separates what is domestic from what is not' David Bellos, *Sebald Lecture 2020: 'The Myths and Mysteries of Literary Translation'*, British Centre for Literary Translation, Norwich, UK, attended via Zoom on 29 June 2020.

'Now what food do we feed women as artists upon? . . .' Virginia Woolf, *A Room of One's Own*, Hogarth Press, London, UK, 1929, p. 80.

'In the sixteenth century there was a widespread belief . . .' Sabrina Orah Mark, 'Rapunzel, draft one thousand', *Paris Review*, no. 6, 6 August 2020, <www.theparisreview.org/blog/2020/08/06/rapunzel-draft-one-thousand/>.

'a critic and a skeptic and a dogmatist and historian and . . .' Nietzsche, trans. Norman, *Beyond Good and Evil*, [Fragment 343], p. 199.

'Best of all was her father's permission . . .' Elizabeth Steele, *Virginia Woolf's Literary Sources and Allusions: A Guide to the Essays*, Garland Publishing, London, UK, 1983, p. 6.

'a fine red aeolian dust . . .' Definition of *bulldust*, from Wikipedia, <en.wikipedia.org/wiki/Bulldust>.

'I had quickly learned . . .' Hermann Hesse, trans. Denver Lindley, 'Life Story Briefly Told' in *Autobiographical Writings*, Picador, London, UK, 1975, p. 56.

'One needs to physically rise . . .' John Kaag, *Hiking with Nietzsche: Becoming Who You Are*, Granta Books, London, UK, 2018, p. 6.

'Art . . . alone knows how to turn these nauseous thoughts . . .' Friedrich Nietzsche, trans. Walter Kaufmann, *The Birth of Tragedy and The Case of Wagner*, Random House, New York, 1967, [Section 7], p. 60.

'It is as if the silkworm . . . *feeling of living* . . .' and 'That through which the individual . . .' Nietzsche, trans. Hollingdale, *The Wanderer and His Shadow* [Fragment 9] in *A Nietzsche Reader*, p. 57.

'the task itself has another will . . .' Nietzsche, trans. Norman, *Beyond Good and Evil*, [Fragment 211], p. 105.

'. . . to create new values – even the lion is incapable of that . . .' Nietzsche, trans. Hollingdale, *Zarathustra*, 'Of the Three Metamorphoses', p. 55.

'For it is selfish . . . Let us therefore *limit* ourselves . . .' Nietzsche, trans. Nauckhoff, *The Gay Science*, Book Four [Fragment 343], pp. 188–189.

Meaningful as a 'bankrupt adjective' William Strunk Jr. and E. B. White, *The elements of style*, 3rd ed., Macmillan, New York, NY, 1979, p. 53.

'People often say that a set of books looks ugly . . .' Kenkō, trans. Keene, *Essays in Idleness*, [Fragment 82], p. 70.

'aut liberi aut libri,' Friedrich Nietzsche, trans. R. J. Hollingdale, *Twilight of the Idols and The Anti-Christ*, Penguin Books, London, UK, 2003.

the horror of inadequacy . . . is a reference to Zygmunt Bauman's *Liquid Modernity*, Polity Press, Cambridge, UK, 2012.

'Sticking with the trouble' is a reference to Donna Haraway's *Staying with the Trouble: Making Kin in the Chthulucene*, Duke University Press, Durham, NC, 2016.

'work that bubbles with generosity . . .' Olivia Laing, *Funny Weather: Art in an Emergency*, Picador, London, UK, 2020, pp. 2–4.

'Maybe because we know we can never correct the absence . . .' Beth Nguyen, 'Apparent', *Paris Review*, no. 232, 2020, <www.theparisreview.org/letters-essays/7513/apparent-beth-nguyen>.

Going and Not Going

'All this about staying where you are, dying, living, being born . . .' Samuel Beckett, *The Unnamable*, Faber & Faber, London, UK, 2010, p. 86.

'Christianity needs sickness . . .' Nietzsche, trans. Hollingdale, *Twilight and Anti-Christ*, Penguin Books, London, UK, 2003, [Fragment 51], p. 179.

'All that Donatello left behind in that city . . .' Giorgio Vasari, trans. George Bull, *Lives of the Artists (vol. 1)*, Penguin Books, London, UK, 1987, p. 183.

'Great talents encourage great incapacities . . .' Sarah Manguso, *300 Arguments*, Picador, London, UK, 2017, p. 61.

'Alcohol is bad for me . . .' *and coffee* 'spreads darkness' Friedrich Nietzsche, trans. Walter Kaufmann, *On the Genealogy of Morals and Ecce Homo*, Vintage Books, New York, NY, 1989, pp. 238–239.

'. . . a thing of beauty, Moran, and a joy forever . . .' Samuel Beckett, *Molloy*, Faber & Faber, London, UK, 2009, p. 172.

'Do you read Nietzsche . . .' and 'To be perfectly honest, yes . . .' David Rutledge and Simon Critchley, in *Philosophy in a nutshell pt. 4: Nietzsche and nihilism*, The Philosopher's Zone [podcast], 25 Oct 2020, <www.abc.net.au/radionational/programs/philosopherszone/nietzsche-and-nihilism/12789426>.

'be ready to burn yourself in your own flame . . .' Nietzsche, trans. Hollingdale, *Zarathustra*, 'Of the Way of the Creator', p. 90.

'Tonight I take it out to the porch and miss you . . .' Sabrina Orah Mark, 'Box Three, Spool Five' in *The Babies*, Saturnalia Books, Philadelphia, PA, 2015, p. 10.

Simon Critchley says that Derrida described Nietzsche's philosophy as a sort of software technology is a reference to Critchley's interview with David Rutledge in *Philosophy in a nutshell pt. 4: Nietzsche and nihilism*.

'brilliant, restless figures . . . savage, haunted account[s] . . .' Olivia Laing, '"Every hour a glass of wine" – the female writers who drank', *Guardian*, 13 June 2014, <www.theguardian.com/books/2014/jun/13/alcoholic-female-women-writers-marguerite-duras-jean-rhys>.

'Suffering makes the imagination weak . . .' Natalia Ginzburg, trans. Dick Davis, 'My Vocation', *The Little Virtues*, Daunt Books, London, 2018, pp. 104–105.

'There's this marvelous moment in . . .' Kate Zambreno, 'Writing postpartum: A conversation between Kate Zambreno and Sarah Manguso', *Paris Review*, 24 April, 2019, viewed 4 October 2022, <www.theparisreview.org/blog/2019/04/24/writing-postpartum-a-conversation-between-kate-zambreno-and-sarah-manguso/>.

'During these ferocious years of parenting . . .' Raymond Carver, 'Fires', *Fires: Essays, Poems, Stories*, Picador, London, UK, 1986, pp. 32–33.

'I was in fact as sick as I have ever been . . .' Joan Didion, 'A Preface: Slouching Towards Bethlehem' in *We Tell Ourselves Stories in Order to Live: Collected Nonfiction*, Everyman's Library, New York NY, 2006, p. 6.

'drifting into the arena of the unwell' is a quote from the film *Withnail and I*, written and directed by Bruce Robinson, HandMade Films, London, UK, 1987.

Returning the books to the shelf: 'the books' include Jenn Ashworth, *Notes Made While Falling*, Goldsmiths Press, London, UK, 2020; Maggie Nelson, *The Red Parts: Autobiography of a Trial*, Graywolf Books, Minneapolis, MN, 2016; and Sarah Manguso, *The Two Kinds of Decay*, Picador, London, UK, 2009.

'Nietzsche writes exclusively for you . . .' David B. Allison, quoted in Babette E. Babich's *Words Like Blood, Like Flowers: Philosophy and*

Poetry, Music and Eros in Hölderlin, Nietzsche and Heidegger, State University of New York Press, Albany, NY, 2006, p. 21.

'Perhaps it is nothing but an urge, an aspiration . . . "I like your style" . . .' Brian Dillon, *Essayism: On Form, Feeling and Nonfiction*, Fitzcarraldo Editions, London, UK, 2017, pp. 40–41.

'We are born, sworn, jealous friends of solitude . . .' Nietzsche, trans. Norman, *Beyond Good and Evil*, [Fragment 44], p. 42.

'The complete woman . . .' Nietzsche, trans. Hollingdale, *Twilight and Anti-Christ*, 'Maxims and Arrows [20]', p. 34.

'stand apart from the rest of the world . . .' Irving Goh, 'Rejecting Friendship: Toward a Radical Reading of Derrida's *Politics of Friendship* for Today', *Cultural Critique*, vol. 79, no. 1, 2011, p. 98.

'*Untimely* is a small and overlooked work in English . . .' Sue Prideaux *I Am Dynamite! A life of Nietzsche*, Random House, New York, 2018, p. 118.

'We are traditionally rather proud of ourselves . . .' Toni Morrison quoted by Jean Strouse in 'Toni Morrison's Black Magic' profile in 'Books' section of *Newsweek*, 30 March, 1981, p. 53.

'The literary woman, unsatisfied, agitated . . .' Nietzsche, trans. Hollingdale, *Twilight and Anti-Christ*, p. 94.

'I want a lost and found in my living room' Sabrina Orah Mark, 'We didn't have a chance to say goodbye', *Paris Review*, 14 January 2021, <www.theparisreview.org/blog/2021/01/14/we-didnt-have-a-chance-to-say-goodbye/>.

'I may not know how to seduce but I will dazzle . . .' María Negroni, trans. Anne Twitty, 'Islandia', *Paris Review*, no. 130, 1994, <www.theparisreview.org/poetry/1852/islandia-maria-negroni>.

Beckett's autologie créatrice *and* les deux besoins, see Samuel Beckett, 'Les Deux Besoins' in *Disjecta: Miscellaneous Writings and a Dramatic Fragment*, Grove Books, New York, NY, 1984, and John Pilling, 'On Not Being There: Going On Without in Beckett' in *Beckett and Nothing*, Manchester University Press, Manchester, UK, 2020, p. 23.

'. . . friendly obligation or economic need . . .' Samuel Beckett, quoted in Ruby Cohn's 'Foreword' to *Disjecta*, p. 7.

'At a venture one would say that women's books . . .' Woolf, *A Room of One's Own*, p. 117.

'Since 1945 I have written only in French . . .' Samuel Beckett, in a letter to H. Naumann dated 17 February 1954, *The Letters of Samuel Beckett: 1941–1956*, ed. Georg Craig, Cambridge University Press, Cambridge, UK, 2011, p. 464.

'mal armé' wordplay from Nadia Louar, 'Beckett's Bilingual Explorations' in *The New Samuel Beckett Studies*, ed. J-M Rabaté, Cambridge University Press, Cambridge, UK, 2019, p. 231.

'To Kaun he describes language as a veil . . .' J. M. Coetzee, 'The Young Samuel Beckett' in *Late Essays: 2006–2017*, Penguin Random House, London, UK, 2019, p. 184.

Finding the apartment intact and Beckett writing in French, Enoch Brater, *10 Ways of Thinking About Samuel Beckett: The Falsetto of Reason*, Bloomsbury Publishing, London, UK, 2011, p. 14.

'The redemption in Beckett is so small . . .' Anne Lamott, *Bird by Bird*, p. 200.

'Samuel Beckett has been read since the 1950s as a writer whose work is essentially anti-nihilist in nature' Shane Weller, *Literature, Philosophy, Nihilism: The Uncanniest of Guests*, Palgrave Macmillan, London, UK, 2008, p. ix. See also Alain Badiou cited in Andrew Gibson's *Beckett and Badiou: The Pathos of Intermittency* (2006, p. 130) and Jean-Michel Rabaté's 'Philosophizing with Beckett: Adorno and Badiou' (2010), as well as Theodor Adorno cited in Weller (2008, p. 163).

Beckett denying that the leaf was a symbol of hope: 'Not to show hope or inspiration, but only to record the passage of time' Samuel Beckett, quoted in Deirdre Bair, *Samuel Beckett*, Vintage Books, London, UK, 1990, p. 406.

'I had gained a lot of weight . . .' Dolly Parton, *Songteller: My Life in Lyrics*, Hodder & Stoughton, London, UK, 2020, p. 220.

listening is a philosophical stance, see Jean-Luc Nancy, trans. Charlotte Mandell, *Listening*, Fordham University Press, New York, NY, 2007.

Whatever you say, say nothing, Seamus Heaney, 'Whatever you say, say nothing' in *North*, Faber & Faber, London, UK, 2010.

'I was never elsewhere . . .' Beckett, narr. Barrett, *The Unnamable*.

'Did he love me then? . . .' Beckett narr. Barrett, *Molloy* (in *Molloy, Malone Dies, The Unnamable*, Grove Press, New York, 1955, p. 120).

'One must be mad or drunk . . .' Cioran, trans. Howard, *The Trouble with Being Born*, p. 30.

For more on Beckett's obsession with *going and not going* see Brater, *10 Ways of Thinking About Samuel Beckett*, in particular p. 12.

Jean Anderson in a TV adaptation is a reference to Conor McPherson's 2000 BBC TV adaptation of *Endgame* starring Jean Anderson as Nell.

'Adorno wrote elsewhere . . .' Leland de la Durantaye, *Beckett's Art of Mismaking*, Harvard University Press, Cambridge, MA, 2016, p. 164.

'Everyone looks . . .' Natalia Ginzburg, trans. Dick Davis, 'Silence', *The Little Virtues*, Daunt Books, London, 2018, pp. 113–114.

'. . . will resemble you . . . And there you are . . .' Tristan Tzara's 1920 'dada manifesto on feeble love and bitter love', trans. Barbara Wright, in *Seven Dada Manifestos and Lampistries*, Calder Publications, London, UK, 1977, p. 39.

Beckett 'slumming' Brater, *10 Ways of Thinking About Samuel Beckett*, p. 2.

'I fear we are not . . .' Nietzsche, trans. Hollingdale, *Twilight and Anti-Christ*, p. 48.

'I merely note that I have always been a poor reader . . .' Samuel Beckett, quoted in Dan Gunn,' 'Samuel Beckett' in *Great Shakespeareans: Joyce, T. S. Eliot, Auden, Beckett*, ed. Adrian Poole, 2012, p. 150.

'Estragon: Let's go . . .' Samuel Beckett, *Waiting for Godot*, Faber & Faber, London, UK, 2010, pp. 80–81.

'I said, The sky is further away than you think . . .' Samuel Beckett, *Malone Dies*, Faber & Faber, London, UK, 2010, p. 98.

'Looking up at the blue sky and then at your mother's face . . .' Samuel Beckett, 'Company' in *Company / Ill Seen Ill Said / Worstward Ho / Stirrings Still*, Faber & Faber, London, UK, 2009, p. 5.

'A small boy, stretching out his hands . . .' Samuel Beckett, trans. Richard Seaver in collaboration with Samuel Beckett, 'The end' in *The Expelled and Other Novellas*, Penguin Books, London, UK, 1989, p. 74.

'Regretting – that's what helps you on . . .' Beckett, narr. Barrett, *The Unnamable*.

'Le vent se lève – il faut tenter de vivre . . .' Paul Valéry, 'Le cimetière marin' in *Collected works*, Princeton University Press, Princeton, NJ, 2015, p. 220.

'. . . perhaps that's what I feel, myself vibrating . . .' Beckett, narr. Barrett, *The Unnamable*.

'I couldn't have done it otherwise . . .' Beckett, quoted in Deirdre Bair's *Samuel Beckett*, p. 681.

in the poet's study, silence is turned into objects, reference to W. H. Auden, 'The Cave of Making' in *The Complete Works of W. H. Auden: Poems, Volume ii: 1940–1973*, ed. Edward Mendelson, Princeton University Press, Princeton, NJ, 2022, p. 509.

'to restore silence is the role of objects . . .' Beckett, *Molloy*, p. 10.

'I use the words you taught me . . .' Beckett, *Endgame*, p. 32.

'For all the good . . .' Beckett, *Watt*, p. 249.

'Vladimir: Well? Shall we go? . . .' Beckett, *Waiting for Godot*, p. 91.

Twenty Segments of Waiting

attendre sans s'attendre is a reference to Jacques Derrida as summarised by Goh ('The Derridean strategy, as is well known, is *attendre sans s'attendre*, or waiting without expecting, as Derrida writes in *Foi et Savoir* and many other places') in 'Rejecting Friendship', p. 108.

Moon Overhead, Nothing Moving

'Nihilism is . . . not only the belief that everything deserves to perish . . .' Friedrich Nietzsche, trans. Anthony Ludovici, *The Will to Power*, Book 1: European Nihilism [Fragment 24], Dover Publications, Mineola, NY, 2019, p. 21.

put your shoulder to the plough, Nietzsche, trans. Ludovici, *The Will to Power*, [Fragment 24], p. 21.

'To those human beings who are of any concern to me . . .' Nietzsche, trans. Kaufmann and Hollingdale, *The Will to Power*, Book 4, Part I: Hierarchy [Fragment 910], p. 481.

'Creation – that is the great redemption from suffering . . .' Nietzsche, trans. Hollingdale, *Zarathustra*, 'On the Blissful Islands', p. 111.

Various snippets of Nietzsche condemning the moon and glorifying the sun, Nietzsche, trans. Hollingdale, *Zarathustra*, 'Of Immaculate Perception', pp. 144–147.

'Piously and silently he walks along on star-carpets . . .' Nietzsche, trans. Hollingdale, *Zarathustra*, 'Of Immaculate Perception', p. 144.

First Light

Zarathustra addressing the dawn, the 'blushing sky', Nietzsche, trans. Hollingdale, *Zarathustra*, 'Before Sunrise', pp. 39, 107, 173, 186–187, 333.

we must try to live, 'il faut tenter de vivre . . .' Valéry, 'Le cimetière marin', p. 220.

'Minds grim with nihilism . . .' Christian Bök, 'Chapter I' in *Eunoia: The Upgraded Edition*, Coach House Books, Toronto, ON, 2009, p. 56.

On ne peut penser et écrire qu'assis (G. Flaubert). Now I have you, nihilist!' Nietzsche, trans. Hollingdale, *Twilight and Anti-Christ*, 'Maxims and arrows: [34]', p. 36.

Nietzsche argues that the genuine Christian is the most dangerous nihilist, Nietzsche, trans. Kaufmann, *Tragedy and Wagner*, p. 91.

Nietzsche argues that the genuine Christian harbours anti-artistic sentiments, Nietzsche, trans. Hollingdale, *Twilight and Anti-Christ*, 'Expeditions of an Untimely Man [9]', pp. 83–84.

Nietzsche identifies poetry and creating as that which can redeem us from our suffering, Nietzsche, trans. Hollingdale, *Zarathustra*, 'On the Blissful Islands', p. 111.

Nietzsche calls art the 'highest task", and that which makes life both possible and worth living, Nietzsche, trans. Kaufmann, *Tragedy and Wagner*, pp. 31–32.

Nietzsche refers to himself, as a poet and a philosopher, as both a 'pessimist and art-deifier', Nietzsche, trans. Kaufmann, *Tragedy and Wagner*, p. 25.

Nietzsche offers art as the only truly metaphysical activity of man, that which goes beyond morality, Nietzsche, trans. Kaufmann, *Tragedy and Wagner*, 'Attempt at a Self-Criticism', p. 22.

'It was against morality that my instinct turned with this questionable book, long ago' Nietzsche, trans. Kaufmann, *Tragedy and Wagner*, 'Attempt at a Self-Criticism', p. 24.

'Someone once said . . .' Maxine Kumin, 'How It Was: Maxine Kumin on Anne Sexton', in *The Complete Poems of Anne Sexton*, Mariner Books, New York, NY, 1999, p. xxi.

'the poet's whole conception . . .' Nietzsche, trans. Kaufmann, *Tragedy and Wagner*, p. 68.

'We want to be the poets . . .' Nietzsche, trans. R. Kevin Hill, *The Joyous Science*, Penguin, UK, 2018, p. 307.

Nietzsche's views on poets as liars: see Nietzsche, trans. Kaufmann, *Tragedy and Wagner*; Nietzsche, trans. Hollingdale, *Twilight and Anti-Christ*; Nietzsche, trans. Hollingdale, *Zarathustra*; and Aaron Ridley, *Routledge Philosophy Guidebook to Nietzsche on Art*, Routledge, London, UK, 2007.

Nietzsche aligns himself with art, as life-affirming, as possibility, as becoming, as potential, Nietzsche, trans. Kaufmann, *Tragedy and Wagner*, pp. 21–23.

The joy of dawn now that the 'old God is dead' Nietzsche, trans. Nauckhoff, *The Gay Science*, Book Five [Fragment 343], p. 199.

'But I am leaving you . . .' Nietzsche, trans. Hollingdale, *Zarathustra*, 'Zarathustra's Prologue', p. 52.

The Fertile Abyss

'The challenge, I thought and think . . .' Elena Ferrante, trans. Ann Goldstein, 'Histories, I' in *In the Margins: On the Pleasures of Reading and Writing*, Europa Editions, New York, NY, 2022, p. 80.

'One holds every phrase, every scene to the light as one reads . . .' Woolf, *A Room of One's Own*, pp. 108–109.

we can only take from a text what we already know is a paraphrase of 'Ultimately, no one can extract from things, books included, more than he already knows', Friedrich Nietzsche, trans. R. J. Hollingdale, 'Why I Write Such Good Books', *Ecce Homo*, Penguin Random House, London, UK, 2004, p. 40.

use Nietzsche as a confrontation with ourselves in order to become something else is a paraphrase of Jesús R. Velasco in 'Martin Heidegger's *Nietzsche* (1936–1939)', *13/13 Nietzsche 2016–17*, 29 August 2016, <blogs.law.columbia.edu/nietzsche1313/1-13/>.

'To the question: How do authors of sketches . . .' Robert Walser, trans. Christopher Middleton, 'Poets' in *The Walk and Other Stories*, Serpent's Tail, London, UK, 2013, p. 120.

'If, again, it is asked . . .' Walser, trans. Middleton, 'Poets', p. 120.

'*A revaluation of all values*, this question-mark so black . . .' Nietzsche, trans. Hollingdale, 'Foreword' in *Twilight and Anti-Christ*, p. 31.

the abyss over which the tightrope walker is suspended, Nietzsche, trans. Hollingdale, *Zarathustra*, p. 43.

'the glance plunges *downward* and the hand grasps *upward* . . .' Nietzsche, trans. Hollingdale, *Zarathustra*, p. 164.

Zarathustra must steel himself against his instinct to glance upwards towards the heights whilst also trying to hold onto the depths, paraphrase of Nietzsche, trans. Hollingdale, 'Of Manly Prudence' in *Zarathustra*, pp. 164–166.

'sooner than other mortals and otherwise than they' Martin Heidegger, trans. Albert Hofstadter, 'What Are Poets For?' in *Poetry, Language, Thought*, Harper & Row, New York, NY, 1971, p. 93.

'A story means . . .' George Saunders, *A Swim in a Pond in the Rain: in Which Four Russians Give a Master Class on Reading, Writing and Life*, Bloomsbury Publishing, London, UK, 2022, p. 334.

'How deeply does it reach . . .' Heidegger, trans. Hofstadter, 'What Are Poets For?', p. 96.

'. . . *and what are poets for in a destitute time?*' Friedrich Hölderlin quoted in Martin Heidegger, trans. Albert Hofstadter, 'What Are Poets For?' in *Poetry, Language, Thought*, Harper & Row, New York, NY, 1971, p. 89.

Rilke differentiates between Urgrund, Nature, and Abgrund, abyss in Heidegger, trans. Hofstadter, 'What Are Poets For?', p. 92.

'If that which has been flung . . .' Heidegger, trans. Hofstadter, 'What Are Poets For?', p. 102.

The ventured is unprotected but the venture is its security is a paraphrase of Heidegger, trans. Hofstadter, 'What Are Poets For?', pp. 102–103.

Lahiri's sensual, watery metaphors (pp. 7, 29, 97), going into a foreign language as going into the woods (p. 47), going inward, slowly and hesitantly (p. 91), language as bone and marrow (p. 93) and unable to reach the heart of Italian as its internal, hidden layers elude her (p. 91) are all from Lahiri, trans. Goldstein, *In Other Words*, Bloomsbury, London, UK, 2015.

'Nietzsche hat mich kaputt gemacht' Martin Heidegger, cited by Babette Babich in 'Heidegger's Nietzsche: Virgules, Conjunctions, Being Broken', *Nietzsche 13/13 (2016-17)*, 6 September 2016, <blogs. law.columbia.edu/nietzsche1313/babette-babich-heideggers-nietzsche-virgules-conjunctions-being-broken/>.

'Over the years Venice . . .' Lahiri, trans. Goldstein, *In Other Words*, pp. 99–101.

Irigaray said that she wrote the book 'not in a library or at a desk . . .', according to Kelly Oliver, 'Reading Nietzsche with Irigaray: Not Your Garden-Variety Philosophy', *Journal of French and Francophone Philosophy*, vol. 27, no. 1, 2019, p. 51.

'Ce n'est pas un livre *sur* Nietzsche mais *avec* Nietzsche . . .' Luce Irigaray in an interview with Suzanne Lamy and Andre Roy in *Le corps-à-corps avec la mère*, Éditions de la pleine lune, Montreal, QC, 1981, p. 44.

'It's not a book *about* Nietzsche, but a book *with* Nietzsche . . .' Luce Irigaray, trans. Gemma Parker.

'Et encore trop je vous aime . . .' Luce Irigaray, *Amante Marine*, Les éditions de minuit, Paris, 1980, p. 10.

'And yet I still love you too well in my silence . . .' Luce Irigaray, trans. Gillian C. Gill, *Marine Lover*, Columbia University Press, New York, NY, 1991, pp. 3–4.

'Et n'est-ce oubli de premières eaux . . .' Irigaray, *Amante Marine*, p. 44.

'And isn't it by forgetting the first waters . . .' Irigaray, trans. Gill, *Marine Lover*, p. 38.

'As a writer I can demolish myself . . .' Jhumpa Lahiri, 'Teach yourself Italian', *New Yorker*, 29 November 2015, <www.newyorker.com/magazine/2015/12/07/teach-yourself-italian>.

'. . . In the meantime, however, often I think . . .' Friedrich Hölderlin, trans. Andrew Shanks, '"Bread and Wine" and other poems', *PN Review*, vol. 39, no. 2, 2012, pp. 48–50.

'Long is the destitute time of the world's night . . .' Heidegger, trans. Hofstadter, 'What Are Poets For?', pp. 92–93.

'dizzying yet fertile abyss' Lahiri, trans. Goldstein, *In Other Words*, p. 45.

'Plus bas qu'écorce solide . . .' Irigaray, *Amante Marine*, p. 26.

'Lower than the earth's crust . . .' Irigaray, trans. Gemma Parker.

'The destitution is wholly obscured . . .' Heidegger, trans. Hofstadter, 'What are poets for?', p. 93.

'The Water Rat was restless . . .' Kenneth Grahame, *The Wind in the Willows*, Grosset & Dunlap, New York, NY, 1966, p. 161.

'a self-sufficing animal, rooted to the land . . .' Grahame, *The Wind in the Willows*, p. 163.

'Yet we must think of the world's night as a destiny . . .' Heidegger, trans. Hofstadter, 'What Are Poets For?', p. 93.

'"First," explain the swallows to Rat . . .' Grahame, *The Wind in the Willows*, p. 166.

'A stubborn attempt, a continuous trial' (p. 9); disorienting, disquieting (p. 101); a process that denies shortcuts . . . (p. 91); stubborn (p. 63) and 'a transgression, a rebellion, an act of stupidity' (p. 55) are all from Lahiri, trans. Goldstein, *In Other Words*.

'What if some day or night . . .' Nietzsche, trans. Nauckhoff, *The Gay Science*, Book Five [Fragment 341], p. 194.

'O, Zarathustra, you shall go as a shadow . . .' Nietzsche, trans. Hollingdale, *Zarathustra*, 'The Stillest Hour', p. 168.

'I – did not hear: until at last my abyss stirred . . .' Nietzsche, trans. Hollingdale, *Zarathustra*, 'Of Involuntary Bliss', p. 183.

'the Rat . . . listened fascinated, and his heart burned within him . . .' (pp. 167–168), 'out there, beyond – beyond!' (p. 169), 'Take the Adventure, heed the call!' (p. 180) and *Rat cannot explain what happened to him* (p. 182) are all from Grahame, *The Wind in the Willows*.

'My mother left me a word in her dialect . . .' Elena Ferrante, trans. Ann Goldstein, *Frantumaglia: A Writer's Journey*, Text Publishing, Melbourne, 2016, pp. 89–90.

'Casually then, and with seeming indifference . . .' Grahame, *The Wind in the Willows*, p. 183.

'And it is all my art and aim . . .' Nietzsche, trans. Hollingdale, *Zarathustra*, 'Of Redemption', p. 161.

'Maintain distance, yes, but only then to get as close as possible . . .' Ferrante, trans. Goldstein, 'Histories, I', pp. 80–81.

The female writer must prove 'by summoning, beckoning . . .' Woolf, *A Room of One's Own*, p. 140.

'Over time, writing has come to mean . . .' Ferrante, trans. Goldstein, *In the Margins*, p. 38.

'loose-knit and yet not slovenly . . .' Virginia Woolf, entry from 20 April 1919, in *A Writer's Diary: Being Extracts From the Diary of Virginia Woolf*, ed. Leonard Woolf, Harcourt, San Diego, CA, 2003, p. 13.

English and Italian as duelling siblings . . . Lahiri, trans. Goldstein, *In Other Words*, pp. 114–123.

Blissful Isles

All biographical details of the life of Friedrich Nietzsche are drawn from: Sue Prideaux's *I am Dynamite! A Life of Nietzsche*, Random House, New York, NY, 2018; Paolo D'Iorio, *Nietzsche's Journey to Sorrento: Genesis of the Philosophy of the Free Spirit*, University of Chicago Press, Chicago, IL, 2016; and Paul Bishop, *On the Blissful Islands with Nietzsche and Jung*, Routledge, London, UK, 2017.

'wandering philosopher' D'Iorio, *Nietzsche's Journey to Sorrento*, p. 4.

'I have belonged to solitude too long . . .' Nietzsche, trans. Hollingdale, *Zarathustra*, 'The Child with the Mirror', p. 108.

'[t]he Blessed Isle of Ischia had represented for Nietzsche . . .' Peter Groff, 'Zarathustra's Blessed Isles: Before and After Great Politics', *Journal of Nietzsche Studies*, vol. 52, no. 1, 2021, p. 143.

the Soothsayer, the nihilist prophet, claims that the Blissful Islands no longer exist Nietzsche, trans. Hollingdale, *Zarathustra*, 'The Cry of Distress', p. 256.

Zarathustra declares that his friends and disciples are coming Nietzsche, trans. Hollingdale, *Zarathustra*, pp. 294, 334.

'The fate of Ischia shocks me more and more . . .' Friedrich Nietzsche, trans. and cited by D'Iorio, *Nietzsche's Journey to Sorrento*, p. 79.

Zarathustra's denial, 'No! No! Thrice no!', *declaring that the gloomy prophet knows nothing of these things,* Nietzsche, trans. Hollingdale, *Zarathustra*, 'The Cry of Distress', p. 256.

Zarathustra's overnight trek to the boat . . . Nietzsche, trans. Hollingdale, *Zarathustra*, 'The Wanderer', pp. 173–176.

'cold and deaf for sorrow' (p. 181) *and with* 'riddles and bitterness in his heart' (p. 176) are from Nietzsche, trans. Hollingdale, 'Of Involuntary Bliss' and 'Of the Vision and the Riddle', *Zarathustra*.

'I am again alone and willingly so . . .' Nietzsche, trans. Hollingdale, *Zarathustra*, 'Of Involuntary Bliss', p. 181.

'way that is entirely my own' reference to Nietzsche's letter quoted above, trans. and cited by D'Iorio, *Nietzsche's Journey to Sorrento*, p. 79.

'The signorina must go and rest on Ischia . . .' Elena Ferrante, trans. Ann Goldstein, *My Brilliant Friend*, Europa Editions, New York, NY, 2012, p. 208.

'foolish, but . . . truly mine' Elena Ferrante, trans. Ann Goldstein, *The Story of a New Name*, Text Publishing, Melbourne, 2012, p. 435.

'Ischia does not represent nostalgia and the memory of the past . . .' D'Iorio, *Nietzsche's journey to Sorrento*, p. 5.

The Feeling of Living

'L'art n'est ni le refus total . . .' Albert Camus, *Discours de Suède*, Gallimard, Paris, 1958, p. 54.

'Art is neither the total rejection . . .' Albert Camus, trans. Gemma Parker.

Camus's interest in Nietzsche, documented in Camus, trans. O'Brien, *Resistance, Rebellion and Death* and Robert Zaretsky, *A Life Worth Living: Albert Camus and the Quest for Meaning*, Harvard University Press, Cambridge, MA, 2016.

'I remember hearing the great Spanish poet Rafael Alberti read . . .' Mary Ruefle, 'I remember, I remember', *Poetry Foundation*, 2 July 2012, <www.poetryfoundation.org/poetrymagazine/articles/69829/i-remember-i-remember>.

'Walking is practically and physically beneficial . . .' Kaag, *Hiking with Nietzsche*, p. 27.

'once you begin to hike, it is extremely hard . . .' Kaag, *Hiking with Nietzsche*, p. 29.

All presentation content referenced is from presentations given at *'Blood': A workshop at the University of Adelaide*, Australian Research Council Centre of Excellence for the History of Emotions, 2 November 2020.

'The intelligence of man . . . is nourished not from the gut . . .' Hippocrates, trans. Paul Potter, *Hippocrates vol. ix: Coan Prenotions. Anatomical and Minor Clinical Writings*, Harvard University Press, Cambridge, MA, 2010, p. 67.

'[the heart] nourished in seas of blood which leaps back and forth . . .' Empedocles, trans. Brad Inwood, *The Poem of Empedocles: A Text and Translation with an Introduction*, rev. ed, University of Toronto Press, Toronto, ON, 2001, p. 257.

blood as the seat of reason and understanding was 'totally absurd' Theophrastus, trans. Inwood, *The poem of Empedocles*, p. 195.

The Plague as 'grey and heavy' (Emmanuel Mounier) and 'the dullest of Camus's books' (Georges Bataille) cited in Robert Zaretsky, 'Out of a Clear Blue Sky: Camus's *The Plague* and Coronavirus', *Times Literary Supplement*, 10 April 2020, p. 20.

'. . . all the older forms of literature . . .' Woolf, *A Room of One's Own*, p. 116.

'A mummification of Nietzsche . . .' Penelope Deutscher, 'Irigaray and Nietzsche', *Nietzsche 13/13* (2016–17), 7 April 2017, <blogs.law.columbia.edu/nietzsche1313/10-13/>.

'[T]ell me this . . . I see the spirit of my dead mother . . .' Homer, trans. E. V. Rieu, D. C. H. Rieu and Peter V. Jones, Book 11 in *The Odyssey*, Penguin Books, London, UK, 1991, p. 163.

'You can guess how fundamentally melancholy and despondent I am . . .' Nietzsche in a letter to Carl von Gersdorff, quoted in Kaag, *Hiking with Nietzsche*, p. 19.

Where are the women? is a reference to Cynthia Enloe's *The Curious Feminist: Searching for Women in a New Age of Empire*, University of California Press, Berkeley, CA, 2004.

'the maternal waters out of which all humans are born . . .' Oliver, 'Reading Nietzsche with Irigaray', p. 51.

For Arendt, Nietzsche's weakness is his solitude . . . is a summary of ideas from Hannah Arendt's, *The Life of the Mind: Volume Two, Willing*, Harcourt Brace Jovanovich, New York, NY, 1978; these ideas are also explored in 'Arendt on Willing', *Nietzsche 13/13 (2016–17)*, 15 November 2016, <blogs.law.columbia.edu/nietzsche1313/5-13/>.

'a critic and a skeptic and a dogmatist and historian and . . .' Nietzsche, trans. Norman, *Beyond Good and Evil*, [Fragment 343], p. 199.

'J'aime cette vie avec abandon . . .' Albert Camus, 'Noces à Tipasa', *Noces: suivi de l'été*, Gallimard, Paris, 1959, p. 18.

'I love this life with abandon . . .' Albert Camus, trans. Gemma Parker.

'Contrairement au préjugé courant . . .' Camus, *Discours de Suède*, p. 42.

'Contrary to popular opinion . . .' Camus, trans. Gemma Parker.

'Only ideas won by walking are of any value' Nietzsche, trans. Hollingdale, *Twilight and Anti-Christ*, 'Maxims and arrows: [34]', p. 36.

'*Sit* as little as possible.' Nietzsche, trans. Kaufmann, *Morals and Ecce Homo*, 'Why I Am So Clever', pp. 239–240.

the West 'mishandles' *its culture*; 'She might have looked elsewhere . . .' Anonymous, 'Why so many love the philosophy of the East, and so few that of the West', *School of Life*, n.d., <www.theschool oflife.com/thebookoflife/east-and-west-philosophy/>.

'. . . le mélange des souffles avec qui je n'ai pas choisi me déplait . . .' Irigaray, 'Ecce mulier? Fragments', p. 144.

'It bothers me to mix my breath with someone I have not chosen . . .' Irigaray, trans. Gemma Parker.

'Le monde est beau, et hors de lui, point de salut' Camus, 'Le désert' in *Noces*, p. 70.

'The world is beautiful, and outside of it, there is no salvation' Albert Camus, trans. Gemma Parker.

'The key to their effectiveness . . .' John Brookfield, quoted in Michael Easter and Trevor Reid, 'A Beginner's Guide to Battling Ropes: When You Want to Pack on Lean Mass, Pick up a Rugged Rope', *Men's Health*, 21 May 2018, <www.menshealth.com/fitness/a19537513/how-to-use-battling-ropes/>.

'I believe that reading in a foreign language is the most intimate way of reading' Lahiri, trans. Goldstein, *In Other Words*, p. 43.

'Et soudain, sans transition . . .' Albert Camus, *La Peste* in *Théâtre, Récits, Nouvelles*, Gallimard, Paris, 1962, p. 1266.

'Suddenly, unexpectedly . . .' Albert Camus, trans. Gemma Parker.

'Then suddenly, with no stopping halfway . . .' Albert Camus, trans. Robin Buss, *The Plague*, Penguin Classics, London, 2013, p. 46.

'à mi-distance de la misère et du soleil' Albert Camus, *Essais*, Gallimard, Paris, 1965, p. 6.

somewhere between poverty and the sun, Albert Camus, trans. Gemma Parker.

'I realized later that there was probably nothing more disobedient . . .' Alice Notley, 'The Poetics of Disobedience', *Poetry Foundation*,

15 February 2010, <www.poetryfoundation.org/articles/69479/the-poetics-of-disobedience>.

Walter Kaufmann's dedication of *The Birth of Tragedy* in Nietzsche, trans. Kaufmann, *Tragedy and Wagner*.

'écrasé et exalté en même temps . . .' Camus, *Discours de Suède*, p. 68.

'both crushed and elevated . . .' Camus, trans. Gemma Parker.

'J'ai souvent . . .' Camus, *Discours de Suède*, pp. 68–69.

'I have often . . .' Camus, trans. Gemma Parker.

'Camus said that the only true function of man . . .' William Faulkner, 'Albert Camus', *The Transatlantic Review*, no. 6, 1961, p. 5.

Nietzsche was 'perpetually sick'; felt good 'at best one day in ten' Erich Heller, 'Nietzsche's Terror: Time and the Inarticulate', *Salmagundi*, nos. 68/69, 1985, p. 79.

'Sickness *detached me slowly* . . .' Nietzsche, trans. Kaufmann, *Morals and Ecce Homo*, 'Why I am So Clever', pp. 287–288.

'creation of freedom for oneself and a sacred "No" even to duty' Nietzsche, trans. Hollingdale, *Zarathustra*, 'Of the Three Metamorphoses', p. 55.

'The island. A last effort . . .' Beckett, *Malone Dies*, p. 117.

'I now think that if literature written by women . . .' Ferrante, trans. Goldstein, 'Histories, I', p. 86.

'La question, pour tous ceux qui ne peuvent vivre sans l'art . . .' Albert Camus, *Discours de Suède*, pp. 28–29.

'The question, for those who cannot live without art . . .' Camus, trans. Gemma Parker.

'Late one evening, I stepped out of my little hut . . .' David Abram, *The Spell of the Sensuous: Perception and Language in a More-Than-Human World*, Random House, New York, NY, 1997, pp. 3–4.

Society can only survive if it acknowledges the fundamental violence at the heart of the polis . . . paraphrase of ideas about Dionysus and Pentheus by Terry Eagleton, 'Invitation to an Orgy', *Holy Terror*, Oxford University Press, Oxford, UK, 2005, pp. 6–9.

'Dans la jeune lumière l'hiver sera sec . . .' Albert Camus, *La Postérité du Soleil*, Gallimard, Paris, 2020, p. 30.

'In the young light of the sun, winter will be dry . . .' Albert Camus, trans. Gemma Parker.

Kant's mechanical, strolls throughout his hometown of Königsberg is a reference to Kaag, *Hiking with Nietzsche*, p. 44.

'This nihilist with his Christian dogmatic entrails . . .' Nietzsche cited in Kaag, *Hiking with Nietzsche*, p. 45.

'a kind of freedom one can't go at or for directly . . .' Maggie Nelson, 'Drug Fugue' in *On Freedom*, Jonathan Cape, London, UK, 2021, p. 167.

'This is precisely what happens . . .' Ferrante, trans. Goldstein, 'Histories, I', p. 78.

'Because fear is good for the soul? . . .' Nancy Lemann, 'Diary of Remorse', *Paris Review*, no. 241, 2022, <www.theparisreview.org/fiction/7913/diary-of-remorse-nancy-lemann>.

'La pauvreté . . . n'a jamais été un malheur pour moi . . .' Camus, *Essais*, p. 6.

'Poverty . . . was never a source of unhappiness . . .' Albert Camus, trans. Gemma Parker.

'What leads to a true understanding of Nietzsche . . .' Karl Jasper, *Nietzsche: An Introduction to the Understanding of His Philosophical Activity*, John Hopkins University Press, 1997, p. 9.

'For – believe me – the secret . . .' Nietzsche, trans. Nauckhoff, *The Gay Science*, Book Four [Fragment 283], p. 161.

'From the creative point of view there is nothing so dangerous as security' Lahiri, trans. Goldstein, *In Other Words*, p. 85.

'an awareness of impossibility is central to the creative impulse' Lahiri paraphrasing Fuentes, trans. Goldstein, *In Other Words*, p. 93.

'Presently the tactful Mole slipped away . . .' Grahame, *The Wind in the Willows*, p. 183.

'il faut tenter de vivre . . .' Valéry, 'Le cimetière marin', p. 220.

'L'immortalité de l'âme . . .' Camus, 'Le désert', p. 59.

'The immortality of the soul . . .' Camus, trans. Gemma Parker.

'privileged site of resistance . . .' Weller, *Literature, Philosophy, Nihilism*, p. 22.

'You say "I" and you are proud of this word . . .' Nietzsche, trans. Hollingdale, *Zarathustra*, 'Of the Despisers of the Body', p. 62.

'If that which has been flung . . .' Heidegger, trans. Hofstadter, 'What Are Poets For?', p. 102.

'It is an excellent thing to express . . .' Nietzsche cited in Kaag, *Hiking with Nietzsche*, p. 223.

'Chaque artiste garde ainsi . . .' Albert Camus, 1970, *L'envers et l'endroit*, Gallimard, Paris, p. 13.

'Each artist therefore carries . . .' Camus, trans. Gemma Parker.

Acknowledgements

I received financial support to write this book from an Australian Government Research Training Program stipend and an independent artists grant from CreateSA, and guidance in my writing and research from a PhD position at the University of Adelaide as part of the J. M. Coetzee Centre for Creative Practice. I wish to acknowledge and thank all those who provided feedback and advice during my time as a postgraduate, with particularly heartfelt thanks to Jennifer Rutherford, Anna Goldsworthy, Patrick Flanery, and Clare Charlesworth. This project was also supported by a Varuna Residential Fellowship in the Blue Mountains and time at Island View Writers' House in Clayton Bay.

I thank the publishers and editors of the journals in which fragments and essays from this work have appeared, including *Meanjin*, *Meniscus* and *Transnational Literature*. I also want to thank the organisers of the public readings at which I read early versions of this work, including the Life Narrative Lab's 'Lives in Motion' event, 'Thinking Writing Now' at Adelaide Writers' Week, the No Wave 'Poetry in Translation' night, postgraduate conferences in the English, Creative Writing and Film Department at the University of Adelaide, and as a featured writer at the literary salon Dog-Eared Readings.

The brilliant Patrick Flanery deserves thanks twice, as this book would not exist without his robust support, nor without the wisdom of my publisher, Ben Ball, and my fearless editor, Lizzie Levot. I also wish to warmly thank the estate of the iconic Agnès Varda for the permission to use the photo on the front cover, and Alissa Dinallo for the gorgeous design.

On a personal note, I'd like to thank my mum and dad for being courageous, unusual and interesting people, for loving me and for giving me permission to use their stories. I'd also like to thank the many friends and relatives who lent their voices and lives to my project over the years. Finally, I am forever thankful for, and inspired by, the regular good-humour and reckless creative energy of the artists I live with: my husband, Guillaume, my daughter, Anouk, and my son, Noé.

About the Author

Gemma Parker is a poet and essayist, teaching creative non-fiction at Adelaide University. She has lived, worked and studied in Osaka, Paris, London and Hanoi.

Find Gemma at gemma-parker.com.